LEE CANTER'S

ASSERTIVE DISCIPLINE

Positive Behavior Management for Today's Classroom

NEW AND REVISED
4TH EDITION

Solution Tree | Press

a division of
Solution Tree

555 North Morton Street
Bloomington, IN 47404

800.733.6786 (toll free) / 812.336.7700
FAX: 812.336.7790

email: info@solution-tree.com
solution-tree.com

Printed in the United States of America

18   17   16   11   12   13   14   15

Library of Congress Cataloging-in-Publication Data

Canter, Lee.
  Lee Canter's assertive discipline : positive behavior management for today's classroom / Lee Canter. -- 4th ed.
      p. cm.
  Cover title: Lee Canter's assertive discipline
  Includes bibliographical references and index.
  ISBN 978-1-934009-15-4 (perfect bound : alk. paper) -- ISBN 978-1-935249-23-8 (library binding : alk. paper) 1. School discipline. 2. Behavior modification. 3. Classroom management. I. Title. II. Title: Lee Canter's assertive discipline.
  LB3013.C33 2010
  371.102'4--dc22
                          2009034667

Solution Tree
Jeffrey C. Jones, CEO & President

Solution Tree Press
President: Douglas M. Rife
Publisher: Robert D. Clouse
Director of Production: Gretchen Knapp
Managing Production Editor: Caroline Wise
Senior Production Editor: Suzanne Kraszewski
Proofreader: Elisabeth Abrams
Text Designer: Amy Shock

Cover Designer: Pamela Rude

This book is dedicated to all the educators at Aspire Public Schools. Your commitment has inspired me to redouble my efforts to do all in my power to help to close the achievement gap in our nation's schools.

Acknowledgments

This book would not exist if it were not for the vision and persuasive skills of Douglas Rife, president of Solution Tree Press. As well, I appreciate the efforts of Gretchen Knapp and the editorial staff at Solution Tree for helping make this book a reality.

In addition, to my wife, Barb, for all the time and effort she put in to editing the manuscript—you're simply the best!

Finally, thank you to all the educators I have the privilege to work with each day who strive diligently to provide a high-quality education to our country's youth.

Solution Tree gratefully acknowledges the contributions of the following reviewers:

Anne Gregory
Assistant Professor, Clinical and School Psychology
Curry School of Education, University of Virginia
Charlottesville, Virginia

Amanda Bozack
Assistant Professor
University of New Haven
West Haven, Connecticut

Dave Levin
Cofounder
KIPP Schools
New York, New York

Dennis Wiseman
Professor
Spadoni College of Education, Coastal Carolina University
Conway, South Carolina

Janet Robinson
Superintendent
Newton Connecticut Public Schools

Robert J. Marzano
CEO
Marzano Research Laboratory
Englewood, Colorado

Table of Contents

About the Author ———————————————————————————— xi

Introduction ————————————————————————————————— 1

Section One: Becoming an Effective Classroom Manager

1: You Can Be an Effective Classroom Manager ——————————————— 3
Why Is Classroom Management Such a Significant Issue for Today's Teachers? ————— 3
Why Are Some Teachers Such Effective Classroom Managers? ————————————— 5
You Can Learn to Be an Effective Classroom Manager ——————————————— 6

2: Develop Your Teacher Voice ——————————————————————— 9
Attributes of the Teacher Voice ———————————————————————— 9
Building Your Teacher Voice ————————————————————————— 13

3: Hold High Expectations ————————————————————————— 15
Expect 100 Percent Compliance With Your Directions 100 Percent of the Time ———— 15
Allow No Excuses for Disruptive Behavior —————————————————— 16
Always Sweat the Small Stuff ————————————————————————— 17
Never Back Down —————————————————————————————— 18
Let Students Know You Are Not Going Away ———————————————————— 18
Avoid Excessive Praise ———————————————————————————— 19
The Lesson of High-Stakes Testing Days ————————————————————— 20

Section Two: Developing Your Classroom Discipline Plan

4: Establish Rules ——————————————————————————————— 23
Advantages of Using a Classroom Discipline Plan ———————————————— 24
Developing Your Rules ————————————————————————————— 25

5: Determine Positive Support Strategies ———————————————————— 27
Positive Support for Individual Students ————————————————————— 27
Classwide Positive Support: Points on the Board ————————————————— 29

6: Determine Corrective Actions ——————————————————————— 33
Why You Need to Take Corrective Actions ———————————————————— 33
Guidelines for Planning the Use of Corrective Actions —————————————— 34
Before You Implement Your Classroom Management Plan —————————————— 37

Section Three: Teaching Responsible Behavior

7: Teach Policies and Procedures at the Beginning of the School Year —————————— 39
Determine Policies and Procedures ——————————————————————— 39
Planning to Teach a Lesson on Responsible Behavior ——————————————— 41
Responsible Behavior Lesson Format —————————————————————— 44

8: Develop a Responsible Behavior Curriculum —————————————————— 47
Determine the Order in Which You Will Teach the Content ————————————— 47
Sample Responsible Behavior Curriculums ————————————————————— 48

Section Four: Utilizing the Behavior Management Cycle

9: Effectively Communicate Explicit Directions —————————————— 57
The Behavior Management Cycle ——————————————————— 57
Step One: Clearly Communicate Explicit Directions ————————————— 58

10: Utilize Behavioral Narration ————————————————————— 63
The Trap of Responding to Off-Task Students ————————————————— 63
Behavioral Narration ———————————————————————— 63
Utilizing Behavioral Narration to Motivate Students to Get On Task ———————— 67
Utilizing Behavioral Narration to Keep Students On Task During Instructional Activities ——— 69
Behavioral Narration Is No Substitute for Effective Instruction —————————— 70

11: Take Corrective Actions ————————————————————— 71
Guidelines to Take Corrective Actions in Your Classroom ——————————— 71
How Students Will Test You ———————————————————— 74

12: Teach Students to Manage Their Own Behavior ——————————— 81
The Levels of Classroom Management Structure ——————————————— 81
Level One: Highly Structured ————————————————————— 82
Level Two: Moving Toward Self-Management ————————————————— 84
Level Three: Student Self-Management ——————————————————— 85
Recalibrate ——————————————————————————— 86

Section Five: Reducing Disruptive Behavior

13: Instructional Strategies That Reduce Disruptive Behavior —————————— 89
How to Provide Opportunities to Respond ————————————————— 89
Opportunity to Respond Strategies ———————————————————— 90
Additional Strategies to Engage Students and Reduce Disruptive Behavior ——————— 96

Section Six: Working With Difficult Students

14: Build Positive Relationships With Students ———————————————— 103
The Trust Issue ————————————————————————— 103
Steps to Earn the Trust of All Your Students ———————————————— 105

15: Develop Individualized Behavior Plans —————————————————— 115
Guidelines to Developing an Individualized Behavior Plan ——————————— 115

16: You Can't Do It on Your Own: Getting the Support You Need
    to Deal With Difficult Students ———————————————————— 119
The Myth of the Good Teacher ————————————————————— 119
Initial Steps to Obtain Support From Parents and Administrators —————————— 120
The Importance of Parental Support ——————————————————— 122
Building Positive Relationships With Parents ————————————————— 122
Home–School Behavior Contract ———————————————————— 126
Pulling It All Together ———————————————————————— 127
The Importance of Getting Support From Your Administrators —————————— 127

Appendix

Mentors, Coaches, and School Leadership Teams:
    Structures to Support Classroom Teachers' Behavior Management Efforts ————— 131

1: An Introduction to the Real Time Classroom Coaching Model ——————— 133

The Birth of the Real Time Classroom Coaching Model ————————————— 133

Real-Time Feedback ————————————————————————————————— 137

Advantages of the Real Time Classroom Coaching Model ——————————— 140

Supporting Struggling Teachers ————————————————————————— 142

2: An Introduction to Establishing a Schoolwide Assertive Discipline Program ————— 143

Why So Many Schools' Behavior Management Efforts Are Ineffective ——————— 143

Schools Can Transform Their Learning Climate ——————————————————— 146

Attributes of Schools With Effective Schoolwide Behavior Management Efforts ——————— 146

References and Resources ———————————————————————————— 155

Index ————————————————————————————————————— 161

About the Author

Lee Canter is a world-renowned expert on classroom management. His acclaimed Assertive Discipline® program has been the gold standard in the field since it was first published in 1976. Lee continues to develop cutting-edge coaching and training focused on establishing safe and orderly school environments that support closing achievement gaps. Known as one of the most dynamic speakers and trainers in education today, he has keynoted countless conferences and has been a frequent guest on noted television programs including *The Oprah Winfrey Show,* the *TODAY Show,* and *Good Morning America.*

Cofounder of Canter and Associates, Lee has written more than forty books and training programs for educators, including *Assertive Discipline*®, *Parents on Your Side*®, *Succeeding With Difficult Students*®, *The High-Performing Teacher,* and *Classroom Management for Academic Success.* In addition, he is known for developing one of the most successful distance learning master's programs for educators. Lee and his staff have trained more than one million teachers worldwide in his Assertive Discipline programs.

Lee earned a bachelor's degree in history from California State University, Northridge, and a master's degree in social work from the University of Southern California.

Introduction

It has been more than thirty years since the original *Assertive Discipline* was published in 1976. Since that time, over 1.5 million educators have used the concepts first presented in that book to help create positive learning environments for their students.

Throughout the years, I have continued to go into schools and classrooms and meet with educators using my program. With their feedback and the insights gained from that feedback, I have been able to clarify which strategies are the most effective and have adjusted the program to meet the changing needs of educators and students.

For many years, I have dedicated the vast majority of my efforts to working with beginning and struggling teachers, particularly in the most socioeconomically disadvantaged areas of this country. I see, day in and day out, the challenges these teachers face when attempting to deal with the behavior of difficult students, but often lacking the skills necessary to be successful.

Thus, in this edition, I place particular emphasis on addressing the needs of new and struggling teachers to give them the skills and confidence necessary to take charge of their classrooms in a firm, fair, and positive manner. In order to accomplish this goal, I introduce new concepts, including how teachers can earn the respect of today's students by developing what I call a strong "teacher voice," and provide a step-by-step model for how teachers can teach students to manage their own behavior.

Also you will find included in this edition basic instructional strategies that are vital to help teachers reduce disruptive behavior. The reality is that the more effective the teachers' instruction, the more students will stay engaged and not become disruptive.

I have also incorporated updated versions of concepts that were originally presented in my book *Classroom Management for Academic Success* (2006). These concepts include the Behavior Management Cycle, a fundamental strategy to teach students to follow directions, as well as a Responsible Behavior Curriculum, to guide efforts to teach students appropriate behavior at the beginning of the year. Concepts and strategies from the previous edition of *Assertive Discipline* (2001a) that educators and researchers have validated as being best practices in classroom management are included as well.

Finally, it has become abundantly clear to me that the first step in improving teachers' classroom management skills is to give them the concepts and strategies they need to do their jobs. The reality is, though, that more steps are needed to ensure teachers have the necessary supports to maximize their ability to help students learn to behave responsibly in the classroom.

To begin this process, I've included an appendix in this edition that will provide an introduction to two critical steps to help increase teachers' success:

1. **The Real Time Classroom Coaching Model**—A new model of coaching teachers that enables mentors, coaches, and others to assist teachers with raising their level of mastery in the use of classroom management skills

2. **Establishing a Schoolwide Assertive Discipline Program**—A model for school leadership teams to use to establish a schoolwide behavior management program that supports teachers' classroom efforts

It is my profound hope that as a new generation of teachers begins their efforts on behalf of our youth, they will be empowered by the concepts and strategies in this text as they strive to meet their professional goals and the needs of today's students.

You Can Be an Effective Classroom Manager

You can establish a classroom environment in which you teach and students learn free from the distraction of disruptive student behavior!

How can I make such a bold statement not knowing you or your students?

Over the last thirty years, my staff and I have worked with more than one million teachers at all grade levels and from all types of socioeconomic backgrounds, and we have learned firsthand that any motivated teacher can develop the skills and confidence needed to teach his or her students how to behave.

If you are ready to join this enormous contingent of educators who have learned to successfully manage their students' behavior, then please continue reading.

Why Is Classroom Management Such a Significant Issue for Today's Teachers?

If you are reading this book, you are either struggling with managing student behavior or concerned that you will soon be facing this issue.

Trust me, you are not alone.

> Seventy-seven percent of teachers admit that their teaching would be more effective if they did not have to spend so much time dealing with disruptive students (Public Agenda, 2004).
>
> Fifty percent of teacher time is spent dealing with the disruptive behavior in many classrooms at all grade levels (Cotton, 1990; Walker, Colvin, & Ramsey, 1995).
>
> Forty percent of teachers spend more time keeping order than teaching (Johnson, 2004).

Why do so many teachers struggle with classroom management issues today? Let's look at the reality they face.

Lack of Respect for Teachers' Authority

In the not too distant past, teachers had instant respect and the authority that came with it simply because they were "the teacher." Society reinforced this authority with the high esteem in which it held educators.

Parents reinforced this authority by stressing the importance of education and the importance of listening to the teacher. Students knew that if they got in trouble at school, they'd be in twice as much trouble at home.

Classroom management, or discipline, usually consisted of nothing more than a teacher's stern look or a few well-chosen words. The simple promise "I will call your parents if you do that again" was sufficient to motivate most students, including the most disruptive ones, to choose to behave.

Today the reality you face is quite different. You have to deal with society's lack of respect for teachers and the educational establishment in general. Parents often don't automatically support your efforts and, in fact, many openly question and undermine your authority.

Changing Classroom Demographics

Over the years, the composition of classrooms has changed, particularly with regard to greater inclusion of students with special needs. This is primarily the result of the Individuals with Disabilities Education Act (IDEA), most recently amended in 2004 in the wake of No Child Left Behind legislation, passed in 2001, and a reinvigorated Section 504 of the Rehabilitation Act of 1973.

One result is that many students with special needs who in the past would have been taught in separate classrooms are now fully integrated in general classrooms. Inclusion makes demands on teachers to address previously unfamiliar behavioral issues (Algozzine & Ysseldyke, 2006; Jiménez & Graf, 2008).

Another aspect of the new demographics challenge is increasing cultural, racial, and linguistic diversity in today's classrooms. Students come with new expectations and unfamiliar behavior norms based on backgrounds that differ from those of the majority of students in the past.

As a result of this new reality, you, the teacher, must recognize that the discipline approaches that were effective with previous generations of students often do not work in today's classrooms.

Ineffective Classroom Management Training

Over thirty years ago, in the original edition of *Assertive Discipline*, I stated that "teachers do not receive the training they need to deal with disruptive students" (1976, p. 6). Some things never change. Today an overwhelming number of teachers still do not receive the classroom management training they need to deal with their students.

Most teachers are trained in programs that work just fine with "compliant" students. In psychological-behavioral parlance, compliance refers to an individual's willing acquiescence to a request or a demand. In education, compliance also embodies responsiveness to teacher direction, cooperation, and self-control. Basically, compliant students are those who want to please you. These students respond quickly to your positive actions, discipline, or both. Typically, compliant students make up approximately 80–90 percent of most classrooms.

What about the remaining 10–20 percent? These are the students who, for many reasons, are noncompliant.

> *Noncompliant students* are much more interested in doing what they want, when and how they want, rather than pleasing you.

Most teachers report the classroom management training they receive simply does not prepare them to deal effectively with such students. Why is this a significant issue? Consider this question:

> How many disruptive, noncompliant students does it take to lower the academic achievement of an entire class? You know the answer! One.

The result of having one or more disruptive, noncompliant students who you cannot motivate to listen to you can simply be ruinous to your efforts in your classroom.

Why Are Some Teachers Such Effective Classroom Managers?

For more than thirty years, I have been studying one simple question: what are the attributes of teachers who are effective classroom managers?

Why is it that one teacher can have no behavior problems with her sixth-period class when other teachers consider that same class to be the proverbial "class from hell"? Why is it that a fourth-grade teacher has no trouble with the behavior of several "difficult" students who nearly drove their teachers from previous years out of the profession?

Many educators will state that these so-called naturals were born to teach difficult students. Yes, a small percentage of these teachers are uniquely gifted educators, but the vast majority of the teachers I have studied are simply ordinary educators who mastered specific attributes that are needed to effectively manage students in today's classroom.

Let's look at the attributes effective teachers possess.

A Strong Teacher Voice

Effective teachers have developed the "strong teacher voice" needed to manage a group of students. They know how to *assertively* "say what they mean and mean what they say" so that they have the respect and authority needed to take charge of their classroom.

High Expectations for Student Behavior

These teachers know how to demonstrate through their words and actions that they expect all their students to learn to behave appropriately, and they will do whatever it takes to ensure this happens.

An Effective Classroom Discipline Plan

Effective teachers proactively develop a systematic plan—including classroom rules, positive support strategies, and disciplinary consequences—that guides all their classroom management efforts from the first day of school onward.

Policies and Procedures Taught at the Beginning of the Year

The number one priority for these teachers at the beginning of the year is not teaching the three Rs, but rather systematically teaching students the appropriate behaviors needed to be successful in classroom activities.

The Ability to Motivate All Students to Quickly Follow Directions and to Get and Stay On Task

These teachers have mastered research-validated strategies that enable them to motivate all students to get and stay on task so that the classroom is a safe, orderly environment that promotes academic success.

The Ability to Build Trusting Relationships With Their Students

These teachers know the old adage, "Students don't care what you know until they know you care," thus they use best practices to build positive relationships with students, especially those who can be noncompliant or difficult.

The Ability to Gain Support From Parents and Administrators

Master teachers know they can't do it on their own with difficult students, so they develop the skills necessary to get the support they need from the students' parents and administrators.

You Can Learn to Be an Effective Classroom Manager

The most exciting finding from my research is that any motivated teacher has the potential to master the aforementioned attributes of effective teachers and dramatically reduce the disruptive behavior in his or her classroom. Each year I work with teachers who I propose are just like you, and they use the insights presented in this book to take charge of their classrooms in a firm, fair, and positive manner.

You, too, can transform how you deal with your students. I sincerely believe you can become more effective if you are open to the possibility that there are different, more empowering ways to:

- View the potential positive influence you absolutely do have to motivate students to choose to behave in your classroom

- Look at why students are motivated to behave as they do

- Determine how you will choose to respond to your students' behavior

You don't have to be frustrated by your students' behavior. You can establish a classroom environment that lights you up and promotes the academic success of all your students.

Develop Your Teacher Voice

A major challenge for new teachers and those struggling with behavior issues is for them to develop what I call their "teacher voice." When teachers develop their voice, they are able to *assertively* communicate through their words and actions that they are in charge of the classroom; they say what they mean and mean what they say.

> ## Teacher Voice
> When I'm up here teaching, I expect that all students will have their eyes on me and will not be talking so everyone can hear what I'm saying.

Teachers who have not developed their voice often speak in a meek or nonassertive manner, which communicates to their students that they are not confident in their ability to lead the classroom. They are almost asking the students for permission to be the teacher.

> ## Nonassertive Voice
> I'd like everyone to try to pay attention when I'm teaching.

Why is developing your teacher voice so important? Students will never respect or listen to a teacher who does not assert his or her authority in the classroom in a firm, yet caring manner.

Not sure what the teacher voice sounds like? Think about educators you know or have known who were excellent disciplinarians, such as a former teacher, your master teacher, or a current or former colleague. What do or did they sound like when dealing with students' behavioral issues? That was, in all probability, the teacher voice to which I'm referring.

Attributes of the Teacher Voice

To further help you understand the concept of the teacher voice, let's break down what you will see and hear when teachers use their voice.

The Teacher Voice Has an Assertive Tone

Teachers who have developed their voice assertively communicate their behavioral expectations to their students. By assertive, I mean they speak in a decisive, firm, self-assured manner that leaves no question in the students' minds as to who is running the classroom.

> ### Assertive Tone
> It is time for silent reading. I expect everyone to immediately take out your book and read for fifteen minutes without any talking.

Many teachers confuse having an assertive tone with being controlling or hostile. Let me elaborate on the differences: the tone of the voice is firm, yet caring and should communicate to students the simple message that "I care too much about you reaching your full potential in my classroom to allow any student to stop you from learning or me from teaching for any reason."

The motivation for teachers to use the voice comes from their heartfelt belief that there is no way they will be able to help students be successful unless and until they can establish their authority as the leader of the classroom.

On the other hand, some teachers do speak in a hostile, controlling manner. They are often motivated by their need to stay in control in the classroom, rather than to help the students.

> ### Hostile Tone
> I'm fed up with students being disruptive when I'm up here. If you don't want to learn, that's your problem.

Unlike the firm, yet caring tone of the teacher voice, a hostile tone typically sends the message to students that "I don't like you" or "There is something wrong with you."

The Teacher Voice Fills the Room

When you watch teachers who are struggling with student behavior, you often hear them giving directions, providing positive feedback, or correcting inappropriate behavior in a "weak" voice that does not project authority throughout the classroom.

When you use your teacher voice, you will want to make sure you project your voice so that every student, even those in the far corner of the room, will, without question, be able to clearly hear each and every word you have to say. You want your students to know by your volume, as well as tone, that when you speak, they need to pay attention—period.

The Teacher Voice Never Speaks Over Students

Teachers with the voice will never speak when a student is not paying attention or is speaking out; they expect total silence when they are speaking.

If a student talks when you are talking, immediately stop in midsentence and let the student know that what he or she is doing is unacceptable:

> *Jonas, when I'm speaking, I expect everyone to be silent and pay attention to me. You have chosen to receive the next consequence from our discipline plan.*

Never attempt to teach when students are not paying attention or are speaking to one another. That sends the clear message to your students that "you don't have to listen to me!"

The Teacher Voice Is Used When Recognizing Appropriate Student Behavior

Most educators associate the need to use the teacher voice with when they are dealing with students' disruptive behavior. On the contrary, effective teachers have learned that it is equally, if not more, important to use the voice when recognizing students' appropriate behavior. Why?

The most effective way to assert your authority is by constantly monitoring student behavior and letting them know you are doing so by singling out students who are meeting your expectations. Thus, in a firm voice that fills the room, you would want to constantly make statements such as this:

> *I see James, Juanita, and Tyrone are paying attention with their eyes on me and are not talking.*

The Teacher Voice Is Used When Correcting Disruptive Students

Let's look at how teachers use the voice when correcting the behavior of disruptive students. In order to better help you understand this process, let's begin by examining counterproductive responses teachers often make that you will want to avoid.

Ineffective Responses to Avoid

Nagging. Teachers often ineffectively respond to students' disruptive behavior by initially nagging at them to stop.

> *Why are you talking?*
> *How many times do I have to talk to you about your behavior?*
> *Please try to control yourself.*

Students have learned that teachers who nag at them don't mean business and they can continue their disruptive behavior (Jones, 2000).

Threatening. After nagging at the students, ineffective teachers often start threatening.

The next time you talk I'm going to give you detention.
I'm serious. If you disrupt again I'm going to call your parents.

Students also have learned that most teachers' threats are empty, and they keep testing the teachers because they know nothing is going to happen to them if they do so.

Getting Angry. Finally, ineffective teachers end up getting angry with the disruptive students.

That's it. I've had it with you, and I'm sick and tired of your behavior. Get out!

When a teacher becomes angry, students know they "got" the teacher; he or she is out of control and the students lose respect and trust in the teacher.

Always keep in mind that nagging, threatening, and getting angry are responses that will not produce the results you want when you are attempting to deal with students' disruptive behavior. Let's look at what experience and research tell us works best.

The Effective Response: Assertively Restate Your Expectations to Students

When dealing with disruptive students, teachers with the voice will, in a calm, firm manner, simply tell the students what they are to be doing and, if appropriate, the corrective actions (disciplinary consequences) they have chosen to receive by their behavior.

Madison, the direction was to work without talking. You have chosen to get a detention.

Noah, you are to stay in your seat during independent work time. That is your warning for the day.

Such direct communication of your expectations is the most effective way to let students know you are serious about making sure they stop their inappropriate behavior (Walker, Ramsey, & Gresham, 2004).

Teachers With the Voice Will Not Argue With Students

When a teacher with the voice tells a student to do something, you'll never see him or her engaging in a discussion or argument with the student until the student does what the teacher has asked (Canter & Canter, 2001a).

Teacher: Nick, I want you to sit down and get to work on your assignment.

Nick: Why are you picking on me? Heather's not working.

Teacher: Nick, I understand, but I want you to sit down and start your work.

Nick: But why do I have to if other students don't?

Teacher: That's not the point. I still need you to sit down and begin your work.

Nick: You're always on me.

Teacher: Nick, you have a choice. Get to work immediately or you will choose to go to the office.

There obviously may be a time to talk with a student about his or her concerns, but it should never happen during instructional time and, of course, not until the student has complied with the teacher's wishes.

Building Your Teacher Voice

I've talked about the attributes of the teacher voice; now let's look at how you can build yours. There are several steps teachers find effective to help them build their voice.

Observe a Colleague

Watch a fellow teacher who has good management skills and model his or her tone of voice and mannerisms.

Model After a Teacher You Have Known

Model the voice of an effective disciplinarian you have known well, a former teacher of yours, your master teacher, or a former colleague you have observed.

Get Dramatic

If you feel it is not your style to be assertive, what can you do? Simply go into your classroom and playact having the voice. I have found that teachers who act like they have the voice soon find they are more comfortable than they ever thought they would be with it, and the voice soon becomes part of their teaching persona.

Receive Real-Time Coaching

One of the most effective strategies to help any teacher improve a teacher voice is to receive immediate feedback from a colleague, mentor, coach, or supportive administrator. In the appendix, I discuss the details of how real-time coaching can help you quickly develop your voice.

> ► **Key Points to Remember** ◄
>
> You need to develop your teacher voice to take charge of your classroom.
>
> The teacher voice has an assertive tone and fills the room.
>
> Teachers with the voice never speak over students.
>
> Use your teacher voice when recognizing appropriate student behavior as well as when correcting inappropriate behavior.
>
> Teachers with the voice never argue with students.
>
> Take steps to build your teacher voice.

Hold High Expectations

CHAPTER
3

I'm sure you have heard over and over again that effective teachers have high expectations for their students (Education Trust, 2006; Lane, Givner, & Pierson, 2004). *High expectations* is a vague, esoteric term. I want to give you a clear picture of what teachers with high expectations look and sound like when dealing with student behavior in their classroom.

Expect 100 Percent Compliance With Your Directions 100 Percent of the Time

The cornerstone of what you will see in the classrooms of teachers with high expectations is that they expect and get 100 percent compliance with their directions 100 percent of the time. The bottom line is that 80 percent or 90 percent of the students complying with directions is not acceptable.

Teachers with high expectations basically follow the only commandment of effective classroom management:

> You shall not give a direction to students if you are not prepared to follow through with a disciplinary consequence if they choose not to comply.

Important

Never forget this reality: whenever you tell students what to do, each and every student is watching to see if you will or will not effectively correct the disruptive behavior of any student who does not comply with your wishes.

Thus, if you tell the class, "I need your attention, eyes on me, and no talking," and you start teaching even though some students are not complying with your directions, what are you teaching your students? Basically this: "if you don't listen to me, nothing will happen to you." In other words, students learn they can do what they want and do not have to do what you want them to. Believe me, you're not going to like the fallout if students learn this reality!

On the other hand, though, if you immediately correct—that is, discipline—any students who are not following your directions, you are teaching your students that you expect them to listen to you and you mean business—no exceptions!

To many educators, the thought of expecting all students to follow all directions all of the time sounds rather severe and controlling, and might just set up a power struggle between strong-willed students and an equally strong-willed teacher.

You will never see this potential dynamic in master teachers' classrooms. These teachers, though they are strict by most standards, are equally warm and supportive in their interactions with students. They are not demanding because they are "control freaks." Their motivation comes from the following heartfelt belief:

> Students need to give me 100 percent compliance 100 percent of the time so they can learn to behave in a manner that will maximize their potential to be successful.

A major caveat to all that we're discussing is this:

> If you, the teacher, are expecting 100 percent compliance from your students, you have a responsibility to make sure that 100 percent of your requests are in the best interests of your students.

Again, gaining student compliance is not about power but about serving the best needs of the students. Repeatedly, researchers and practitioners have cited as exemplars schools and individual educators who put into action high expectations. Nowhere is this literature more powerful than in the education of minority and disadvantaged students. Research consistently provides ample evidence that low-performing children of color and those from impoverished homes can succeed when rigorous academics are supported by high expectations (Education Trust, 2006).

Allow No Excuses for Disruptive Behavior

Many students come to class with a multitude of problems: emotional, behavioral, familial, socioeconomic, and so on. Often these students are more difficult to deal with than their peers. Many teachers make excuses for why they allow these "problem" children to disrupt their class.

With the emotional issues he's dealing with, I can't expect him to behave like the other students.

There is no way I can deal with her behavior considering her home environment.

I teach minority students from such a poor, rough neighborhood, how can I ever get them to behave appropriately?

In addition, research indicates that race and gender can also be factors that lead some teachers to hold lower expectations for students' behavior. African American students are frequently held to lower expectations than their non–African American peers. Furthermore, teachers often have even lower behavioral expectations for African American males than females (Strayhorn, 2008).

hold everyone to the same standards. no matter what

In effect, many teachers have two standards of behavior in their classroom: a high standard for students that they view as "normal and compliant" and a lower one for their "problem" students who can't be expected to behave like their "less-troubled" peers.

When you enter the classroom of a teacher with high expectations, you will never see two levels of standards. In these classrooms, there are no excuses for students being disruptive!*

> No students are allowed to engage in behavior that is not in their best interests or the best interests of their peers—for any reason.

These teachers recognize that their students do have real and often heartbreaking problems that can make it harder for them to behave appropriately. They understand, though, the consequences of allowing these students to be disruptive in their classroom. Here is an example of what I mean:

> Adrian is a student being raised by a highly neglectful single mother with a history of drug abuse. In class he is constantly disruptive and often gets upset and angry whenever the teacher disciplines him for not working on the assignments he is capable of completing.

> The teacher soon gets dismayed at seeing how upset and angry Adrian gets, and, rather than providing him with disciplinary consequences whenever he gets upset, she simply tries to calm him down by not demanding he complete his work. Adrian soon begins to fall further behind academically.

Though the teacher's efforts in this example may be well intentioned, allowing troubled students to misbehave ultimately does much more harm than good. When you allow students to disrupt, they will eventually have difficulty in school and will be labeled as a behavior problem. Students like Adrian will not only have to deal with the burden of being raised by a neglectful parent but will, more than likely, have to deal with the additional burden of being a "school failure" as well.

Master teachers know one of the greatest gifts they can give students is to let them know that, despite their problems, they can behave and be successful in the classroom. Such teachers show these students they care enough about them to make no excuses for their disruptive behavior and put in the time and effort to make sure the students meet their expectations in the classroom (Muller, 2001; Watson, 2003).

Always Sweat the Small Stuff

Teachers with high expectations will not let the "small stuff" slide in their classrooms. By *small stuff*, I mean students not paying attention, talking inappropriately, getting out of their seats without permission, playing with a cell phone or iPod®, and so on.

---

* The only obvious exception to this point of view is students with organic problems such as severe ADHD, autism, and so on who are unable to control their behavior.

There is one simple reason this is so important. Master teachers have learned that the more they let students know they are going to firmly deal with the small stuff, the more quickly students learn that the teachers have high standards in their classrooms.

When students learn that you'll not tolerate their doing the small stuff, you'll be creating a classroom environment where they will be much less likely to test you on the serious stuff, such as disrupting your lessons and defying your authority.

Never Back Down

Master teachers do everything in their power to motivate students to choose to behave in a positive manner in their classrooms. There are times, though, that students will make the choice to defy a teacher's authority and disrupt the learning of their classmates:

Teacher: Niguel, you need to stop talking, sit down, and get to work.

Student: Get off my case. I'll work when I'm ready.

These teachers know that if they are to clearly demonstrate their high expectations for student success in their classrooms, they cannot lose such power struggles with a strong-willed, defiant student.

Teacher: Niguel, you have a choice. Immediately get to work, or you're getting a referral to the office.

Student: I don't have to listen to you.

Teacher: I'm sorry you made that choice. Please go to the office now!

Why is being assertive so important when students are defiant? If you allow a student to get away with defying your authority, your power is gone. You will never convince the students you have the high expectations needed to earn their respect and you are basically teaching them that if they get defiant enough, they can do what they want. (In chapter 11, "Take Corrective Actions," I will discuss specific strategies to use with defiant students.)

Let Students Know You Are Not Going Away

Most teachers quickly get frustrated when students don't respond to their classroom management efforts and continually test the limits. These teachers will eventually throw their hands in the air because they believe there is nothing they can do with those students. Students then learn that if they are disruptive, defiant, and strong-willed enough, most teachers will lower their expectations and stop demanding that they behave like the other students.

Master teachers don't play this game. Through their words and actions they send this message to all their students:

"I, the teacher, will do whatever it takes to motivate you to learn to behave and be successful in my classroom—I'm not going away until you do!"

If these teachers' basic classroom management efforts don't work with students, they will change them. For example:

- If students need firmer limits, the teacher will work with the parents, administrators, and others to ensure that under no circumstances will the students be able to get away with disrupting the classroom without firm action being taken to help them learn how to make better choices.

- If students need more positive incentives, the teacher will set up individualized behavior plans to allow the students to earn rewards that will help motivate them.

- If students don't have a positive relationship with the teacher, then the teacher will reach out to the students, spending time getting to know them and their concerns, possibly eating lunch with them, or maybe even going to their homes for a visit.

Students soon learn that master teachers expect all students, no matter how difficult they may be, to learn to behave appropriately and that their teacher will do whatever it takes for this to happen.

Avoid Excessive Praise

Positive reinforcement has the potential to be one of the most potent strategies teachers can use to motivate students. The reality, though, is that ineffective use of this strategy can actually send a message to the students that you really do not have high expectations for how they are to succeed.

The most frequent form of positive reinforcement teachers use is verbal reinforcement. There are two basic types of verbal reinforcement that teachers can give to students: one is recognition, the other is praise. There is a major difference between the two.

Recognition entails letting students know that you acknowledge they are meeting your expectations in a nonjudgmental manner.

> *Jose has his book out, and he is ready to start working.*
> *Marissa is sitting in ready position and paying attention.*

Praise, on the other hand, is judgmental. Along with acknowledging the students have met your expectations, you add comments indicating your approval of their actions.

> *Kaylee has done an excellent job of getting right to work.*
> *I like how Letty is paying attention.*

The Downside of Praising Students for Doing What Is Expected

The harm to students comes from teachers using praise when students simply do what is expected. Let's examine the example of praise just presented: "Kaylee has done an excellent job of getting right to work."

Here is the rub; does the teacher believe Kaylee has been "excellent" by simply getting to work as he has asked? For some teachers, the answer may be yes. They may really be pleasantly surprised that the student did what was asked.

Now let's look at the underlying message this sends to the student.

First off, if the teacher is truly surprised that Kaylee is simply doing what he wants, it indicates that the teacher, in reality, has low expectations for how he expects the student to behave in his class. The message he is communicating to the student is this: "I really don't believe that you will be able to behave like I expect the other students to" and/or "I don't believe I'm capable of getting you to do what I want some or all of the time."

On the other hand, the teacher may not honestly think Kaylee is doing an excellent job by simply getting to work; he is just trying to be a cheerleader who is encouraging the student's efforts. Research and experience demonstrate the impact can be just the opposite.

Studies indicate that students interpret frequent praise as a clear sign that they are doing poorly and need extra encouragement from their teachers (Dweck, 2007). They understand that if the teacher makes a big deal about simply getting to work like the other students, the teacher obviously does not have very high expectations for how they are to perform in the classroom, and students end up meeting the teacher's low expectations by continuing their poor performance.

In addition, teachers who consistently praise students for doing what is expected diminish the importance of their praise and the student behaviors that they really wish to label as "special." In the long run, this diminishes the teachers' ability to truly motivate the students to reach high standards.

I don't want you to take away from this section that you should never praise students. My point is that praise should be reserved for students whose behavior is above and beyond that which you expect of all the students. In chapter 10, "Utilize Behavior Narration," I will elaborate on how and when to provide praise to students.

The Lesson of High-Stakes Testing Days

I think the best way I can illustrate what teachers with high expectations look like is to examine how teachers, probably you as well, deal with student behavior on high-stakes testing days.

Let's start with a question: on days you give mandated achievement tests, how do your students, even those who are difficult, behave? If you're like most teachers, the answer is probably, "Just fine!" My question to you is, "Why?"

> The bottom line on testing days is that you demonstrate through your words and actions that you have high expectations for how the students are to behave.

You expect that 100 percent of your students will comply with 100 percent of your directions. There is no way you're going to allow any of your students to be disruptive during the test without correcting their behavior.

You make no excuses for students acting inappropriately. No matter what kind of problems a student might have, you are not going to let him or her act up during the test.

You sweat the small stuff. Trust me, you are not going to have students talking, or on their cell phones, or listening to their iPods during the test.

Finally, if any student attempts to be defiant for any reason, there is no way you will back down.

On high-stakes test days, you basically "raise the bar" regarding the behavior you expect from your students. You believe what is occurring on test day is so important that the students must cooperate and behave appropriately.

I have some questions for you:

- Isn't what goes on in your classroom every day important to the success of your students?
- Why not raise the bar every day in your classroom?
- If you can establish high expectations on testing days, why not do so on all days?

In the remainder of this book you will be given the strategies you need to help you establish and maintain high expectations for your students.

▶ Key Points to Remember ◀

Expect 100 percent of students to comply with your directions 100 percent of the time.

Make no excuses for why you don't allow inappropriate disruptive behavior.

Sweat the small stuff, especially talking.

Never back down when students are disruptive.

Let students know you are not going away.

Avoid excessive praise.

Have high expectations—not just on high-stakes testing days, but every day.

Establish Rules

A classroom discipline plan is a cornerstone of just about any effective teacher's classroom management efforts. A discipline plan allows you to clarify the behaviors you expect from students and what they can expect in return if they do or do not meet your expectations.

> The goal of a classroom discipline plan is to have a fair and consistent structure that will enable you to establish a safe, orderly, positive classroom environment in which you can teach and students can learn.

A discipline plan consists of three parts:

1. Rules that students must follow at all times *key word!*

2. Supportive feedback that students will receive consistently for following the rules

3. Corrective actions that you will use consistently when students choose not to follow the rules

---

Sample Discipline Plan for Elementary Students

1. Classroom Rules
   - Follow directions.
   - Keep hands, feet, and objects to yourself.
   - No teasing or name-calling.

2. Supportive Feedback
   - Verbal recognition
   - Individual rewards such as the following:
     - ▶ Positive notes sent home to parents
     - ▶ Positive phone calls to parents
     - ▶ Positive notes to students
   - Classroom privileges
   - Classwide rewards

3. Corrective Actions
   - First time a student breaks a rule: Reminder
   - Second time: Five minutes away from group
   - Third time: Ten minutes away from group

---

continued on next page →

- Fourth time: Teacher calls parents with student; student completes behavior journal
- Fifth time: Send to principal
- Severe disruption: Send to principal

Sample Discipline Plan for Secondary Students

1. Classroom Rules
   - Follow directions.
   - Be in the classroom and seated when the bell rings.
   - Use appropriate language; no put-downs or teasing.

2. Supportive Feedback
   - Verbal recognition
   - Individual rewards such as the following:
     - ▶ Positive notes sent home to parents
     - ▶ Privilege pass
     - ▶ Classwide rewards

3. Corrective Actions
   - First time a student breaks a rule: Warning
   - Second time: Stay in class one minute after the bell or lunch detention
   - Third time: Call parents
   - Fourth time: Send to administrator
   - Severe disruption: Send to administrator

Advantages of Using a Classroom Discipline Plan

What will your classroom discipline plan do for you and your students? A discipline plan does the following.

Helps Make Managing Student Behavior More Consistent

A discipline plan helps ensure that you respond to each student in a fair manner. Teachers who do not have a plan tend to react to the students rather than to their specific behavior. Many times a teacher's corrective actions are arbitrary and are based on the history of that student's misbehavior or their mood rather than on the situation at hand. Consider the following example.

> Early in the day, Conner talked out in class, disrupting the lesson in progress. His teacher gave him a reminder and continued her lesson.

> Later that day, Jamie also talked out, interrupting a student who was presenting an oral report. The teacher, visibly annoyed, disciplined Jamie by taking away her recess.

> Finally, at the end of the day, when the teacher was tired and her temper a bit frayed, Bradley talked out. This time the teacher lost her temper, yelled at Bradley, and called his parents that night about his problem behavior.

The teacher's irritated reaction to Jamie and her emotional overreaction to Bradley were unfair and inconsistent. What's more, it most likely created negative tension between the teacher and each student. It will be harder, if not impossible, for them to establish a cooperative relationship in the future.

> Every student has the right to be treated fairly and equally. Every student has the right to the same due process in the classroom. Students need to know that when a rule is broken, they will receive a specific corrective action.

When your students can rely on fair and equal treatment, they will accept your rules and directions more readily, your disciplinary efforts will be more effective, and the groundwork will be laid for you to build positive relationships.

Helps Increase the Likelihood of Parental Support

As I discuss in detail later in chapter 16, "You Can't Do It on Your Own," you need parental support. Before giving that support, however, parents will want to know that you are using a classroom management system that is equitable. Communicating your classroom discipline plan to parents shows them that you care about teaching their children how to behave responsibly.

Helps Ensure Administrator Support

A discipline plan demonstrates to your administrator that you have a well thought-out blueprint for managing student behavior in your classroom. It shows that whenever there is a problem, you will not simply send a student to the office for the administrator to take care of it. Ways to ensure administrative support will be discussed in more detail in chapter 16, "You Can't Do It on Your Own."

Developing Your Rules

Each year brings new students to your classroom. They come with their own needs, their own past school experiences, and their own expectations of teachers. They come with their preconceptions of who you are, what your limits will be, and how they will relate to you and you to them.

Students want to know what expectations you have for them.

> Unless you know how you want your students to behave, how will they know?

Thus, before school begins you want to ask yourself, "What behaviors do I need at all times, each and every day, so that I can teach and my students can learn?"

In answering these questions, most effective teachers come up with the following basic rules:

- **Follow directions.** This is the most important rule you will establish! You can't teach and students won't learn if the many directions you give throughout each day aren't followed.

- **Keep hands, feet, and objects to yourself.** For students to have a safe and orderly classroom, they need to know they are protected from being hit, being kicked, or having their property taken or destroyed.

■ **No swearing, teasing, or bullying.** All students have the right to be in a classroom where they will not be verbally or psychologically abused.

Other rules you often find effective teachers establishing include: (1) no eating, (2) no running in the classroom, (3) do not leave the classroom without permission, and (4) no yelling or screaming.

In selecting your own classroom rules, keep the following points in mind.

Rules Need to Be Observable

Address behaviors that you can clearly see. Unclearly stated expectations may mean one thing to one student and an entirely different thing to another. As a result, they are open to interpretation, are therefore difficult to enforce, and often cause problems by opening the door to arguments. For example:

Observable Rules	Unclear Rules
Keep hands and feet to yourself.	Be respectful to others.
No swearing or teasing.	Be nice.

Rules Need to Apply Throughout the Entire Day or Period

Classroom rules need to be in effect all day or period, no matter what activity is taking place. Avoid rules that may sound sensible but in reality would not be in effect all day, such as, "Raise your hand and wait to be called on before you speak." There are going to be times when students are expected to speak out (for example, in cooperative learning groups). Therefore, this is not an appropriate classroom rule.

Please note: Teachers are often told that they should have the students help determine the rules for the classroom to increase their buy in. While teachers I've studied have, at times, used this process, there is no solid research that indicates getting student input increases student compliance with the rules.

▶ **Key Points to Remember** ◀

A classroom management plan helps make discipline efforts more consistent.

A classroom management plan increases the probability of getting parent and administrator support.

Classroom rules need to be observable and in effect the entire day or period.

Typical classroom rules include the following:

■ Follow directions the first time they are given.
■ Keep hands, feet, and objects to yourself.
■ No swearing, teasing, or bullying.

Determine Positive Support Strategies

CHAPTER
5

These days you must come to class prepared not only to teach subject matter, but also to motivate students to behave appropriately. It is no longer enough to state your expectations and rules. It is also necessary to motivate your students to comply with them.

> Research indicates that teachers who provide effective positive support and feedback reduce disruptive behavior by over 30 percent (Stage & Quiroz, 1997).

As part of developing an effective classroom discipline plan, you need to decide ahead of time what kind of positive support you will use. This means developing a variety of strategies to reinforce the appropriate behavior of individual students as well as the entire class.

Positive Support for Individual Students

The following are the most common positive support strategies to utilize with individual students.

Verbal Recognition

Your number-one choice for positively recognizing student behavior should be verbal recognition. In chapter 10, "Utilize Behavioral Narration," we will discuss one of the most effective forms of verbal recognition, which is a strategy called *behavioral narration*.

Positive Notes and Phone Calls to Parents

Letting your students know that you will send home positive notes to their parents is a great motivator. Just think of its impact. It clearly demonstrates your concern not only about how the student behaves in your classroom, but about your interest in his or her home life as well. Just as important as reinforcing students is establishing a positive rapport with their parents.

> A positive phone call, note, or email is one of the most time-effective means of getting parents on your side because it lets them know you care about their child and want to share in their child's successes.

Dear Mr. and Ms. Lopez,

It is a pleasure to let you know what a terrific job Angel is doing in my class. Every day he works to the best of his ability, and I can always count on him to follow directions and get along with his fellow students. I'm really enjoying having him in my class! You should be proud of the effort he is putting into being a good student.

Sincerely,

Ms. Lund

Behavior Awards

Special awards for good behavior are a form of positive feedback that can be motivating for students of any age. Award certificates usually have a long-lasting effect. Students proudly take them home and post them for the rest of the family to see. Parents report that awards often stay on the refrigerator door for months at a time.

Special Privileges

Allowing a student to participate in an activity he or she particularly enjoys is often a great motivator.

Elementary Special Privileges

Being first in line	Reading a special book
Tutoring younger children	Working on a favorite activity
Being class monitor	

Secondary Special Privileges

Earning extra computer time	Being first out of class
Being excused from one pop quiz	Sitting by a friend for one period
Taking one problem off a test	Correcting papers

Most of your students will respond to verbal recognition, positive notes, or special privileges. You may, however, encounter several students who will not.

Used properly and with careful planning, tangible rewards are effective motivators for those students who are a bit more difficult to reach. It doesn't matter that the reward is a sticker or a snack with little monetary value. What is important is that the student earns a reward that can be seen and touched.

There are going to be times when tangible rewards are really the only positives that will work and the only way you can motivate a student. Some students simply need these rewards to get them back on track. Use tangible rewards, but use them with care.

Classwide Positive Support: Points on the Board

Many teachers find it beneficial to utilize a classwide positive support program with older students (upper elementary, middle, or secondary level), especially at the beginning of the school year or when turning around a difficult classroom. Such a program is one in which all the students work toward earning a positive reward that will be given to the entire class.

One of the most effective classwide reward systems is called "points on the board."

In this system, you establish a goal for the number of points the class must earn to get its reward. Whenever you observe students following your directions, you not only recognize their behavior but, in addition, let them know they have earned a point on the board that will move the class closer to its reward.

> *Juan is going back to his seat, Kris has started working, and Mikayla is working without talking. They have earned a point for the class.*

Points on the Board Enable You to Harness Peer Pressure to Motivate Older Students to Behave

Often middle/secondary students may not want to be singled out for the teacher's attention for fear of being labeled a "kiss up." A powerful advantage of using a points-on-the-board classwide reward system is that it counteracts this fear.

If you enable a student to earn points that will help the class earn a reward they want, the other students will not get on him or her for cooperating. In fact, fellow classmates may encourage the student to keep up the positive behavior. This phenomenon is obviously known as peer pressure.

Savvy teachers utilize peer pressure as a tool to help motive difficult students to choose to behave. These teachers make it a point to constantly monitor those students and make it a goal to ensure they earn more points for the class than the other students. As a result, you often see their classmates egging the difficult student on to behave because he or she seems to be able to earn more points toward the class reward.

Guidelines for Utilizing Points on the Board

Here are the basic guidelines to follow to effectively utilize a points-on-the-board classwide reward system.

Determine the Reward the Class Will Earn

Choose a reward that the students will work toward. Keep in mind this reward must meet two criteria: first, you are comfortable having the students earn it; and second, the students truly want the reward. The following are typical rewards teachers find useful:

- Extra free time
- Extra physical education time

- Special activity
- Class party
- Missing a homework assignment
- Special treat such as popcorn
- Listening to music in class

Make Sure Students Earn the Reward Quickly

It is critical that you make sure your students earn the reward quickly. The number-one reason the points-on-the-board classwide reward system fails to motivate students is because a teacher makes it so hard for the students to earn the reward that they lose interest. The appropriate time span students can wait to earn a reward varies by grade level.

> ### Guidelines for How Quickly Students Need to Earn the Reward
> Grades K–1: One day
> Grades 2–3: Two days to one week
> Grades 4–6: One week
> Grades 7–12: One to two weeks

After the class has earned a reward, determine another reward the class will work toward. You should keep up the use of a classwide reward system as long as you feel the students need an extra incentive that reinforces your behavior-management strategies.

Students Need to Earn Points Frequently Throughout the Day or Period

In order for the points-on-the-board classwide reward system to be motivating, the students have to receive points on a constant basis while in class.

> A good rule of thumb is that students need to earn at least ten points for appropriate behavior per period or hour.

That means you have to be frequently looking for students who are following your directions, narrating their behavior, and giving out points. It may seem like a lot of points, but as long as the goals are reasonable, trust me, the more points you give, the quicker your behavior problems will diminish. Thus, if the students are earning fifty points a day and they, for example, need to earn the reward in three days, the goal the students would need to reach is obviously 150 points.

Never Take Points Away

An important word of warning: never take away points the students have earned. All too often teachers, out of frustration, take away the class' points due to the disruptive behavior of some of the students. This can easily backfire by frustrating the students and, if you are having a particularly bad day, the students can end up not "earning" points, but "owing" points, and believe me, their motivation level will drop.

Establish a "Points Corner" in a Prominent Location

Determine a place on the board where you will record whenever the students earn points. Make sure the location is convenient for you to reach. If appropriate, you can have students record the points when they are earned.

Systematically Introduce the Points-on-the-Board Reward System to the Students

When you decide to use a points-on-the-board reward system, you want to carefully and in detail explain it to the students. You especially want to give middle/secondary students the rationale for why you are using the program, what rewards they can earn, and how they can earn them.

> *I have an idea that I feel can help everyone to learn to follow directions and be successful in this classroom. You have been constantly asking for more free time during class. I have a way for everyone to earn fifteen minutes of extra free time. Here is how it works.*
>
> *Whenever I give directions, I will look for students who are following them. When I see students following directions, I will recognize their behavior and they will earn a point for the class that I will mark here on the board. When the class earns 100 points, you will get fifteen extra minutes of free time at the end of that day.*
>
> *The more I see students following directions, the more points you will earn and the quicker you will get your extra free time.*

When you have finished explaining how the points-on-the-board system will work, take questions from the students to make sure they understand the details of how it will function.

> ▶ **Key Points to Remember** ◀
>
> Planning out how you will provide positive support to students is critical to the success of your classroom management plan.
>
> Determine how you will provide positive support to individual students.
>
> Determine how you will utilize classwide reward programs such as points on the board.

Determine Corrective Actions

We've just discussed how your classroom rules will clearly tell students how they are expected to behave in the classroom at all times, and that consistent use of positive support will help motivate students to follow those rules. There will be times, however, when students will choose not to follow the rules of the classroom. Whenever disruptive behavior occurs, you must be prepared to take corrective action calmly and quickly.

Why You Need to Take Corrective Actions

How to correct or discipline students is definitely one of the more controversial areas in the field of classroom management. Many so-called experts claim that such actions are basically ineffective, if not harmful. When you study effective teachers and look at the research, you will find otherwise.

> Effective use of disciplinary consequences can reduce disruptive behavior in a classroom by close to 30 percent (Stage & Quiroz, 1997).
>
> When used effectively, disciplinary consequences reduce disruptive behavior at all grade levels (Marzano, Marzano, & Pickering, 2003).

Never forget all children deserve structure, and they deserve limits, and allowing them to misbehave is harmful to their success at school. Further, you will again never be able to earn the respect of the students nor be able to effectively take charge of your classroom unless and until you are able to consistently provide students with firm, consistent limits on their inappropriate behavior.

Corrective actions are actions students know will occur should they choose to break the rules of the classroom. Corrective actions must be seen as natural outcomes of inappropriate behavior. They are used to show students that you care too much to allow continued disruptions. Corrective actions are meant to help students realize that their behavior does not serve them, and that it is in their best interests to choose more appropriate behavior.

It must be understood that *corrective* and *coercive* are not synonymous. As discussed previously, coercive discipline, which includes threats, intimidation, and punishment, may *seem* to be effective in the short term, but over time, coercion and "over-explaining" disciplinary actions actually reinforce and increase, rather than decrease, antisocial behaviors, according to a number of authorities (Reid, Patterson, & Snyder, 2002).

Guidelines for Planning the Use of Corrective Actions

Preparation is the key to managing disruptive behavior. By determining in advance what corrective actions you will take when students misbehave, you will have a plan to follow that will allow you to stay in control of every situation. The following are guidelines to use in determining the corrective actions you will include in your classroom plan.

Corrective Actions Should Be Designed to Help Students Learn From Their Mistakes

The goal of corrective actions is not to punish students. You would never punish students for a mistake in reading or math, so why would you punish them when they misbehave? Effective corrective actions are designed to help teach students appropriate behavior.

Corrective Actions Must Be Something That Students Do Not Like, but They Must Never Be Physically or Psychologically Harmful

A corrective action should never be meant to embarrass, humiliate, or physically harm any student. A corrective action will not be effective, though, if the students do not care about receiving it.

Corrective Actions Do Not Have to Be Severe to Be Effective

Teachers often think that the more severe the corrective action, the more impact it will have on a student. This is not true. The key to effective corrective actions is that they are used consistently. It is the inevitability of the corrective action—not the severity—that makes it effective. Here are typical consequences teachers find effective.

1. **Time Out.** Removing a student from the group is an effective corrective action for elementary-age students. Designate a chair or table as the time-out area. Depending on the age of the student, a trip to the time-out area could last from five to ten minutes. While separated from the rest of the class, the student continues to do his or her classwork.

2. **One to Two Minutes After Class.** With older students, simply have them wait one or two minutes after the other students have been dismissed for the next class period or recess. One to two minutes may not seem like a lot of time to you, but it can be an eternity to students who want to walk to the next class with their friends or be the first in line for handball.

   During the one- to two-minute wait, you can take the chance to briefly counsel with the students regarding how you can work together to help them make better choices regarding their behavior.

3. **Think Sheet.** The purpose of a Think Sheet is to encourage the student to think about his or her misbehavior. You may want students to take the Think

Sheet home for parents to sign and return. On the Think Sheet, the student should write down the following:

- The rule that was broken
- Why the student chose to break the rule
- What the student could do differently next time

4. **Miss Free Choice Time.** The majority of students look forward to free time. It is very effective to simply take away part or all of the disruptive student's free choice time.

5. **Recess or Lunch Detention.** Most students would not like to spend part or all of their recess or lunch sitting silently in your classroom. Some schools set up a specific lunch detention for students who have chosen to be disruptive.

6. **Time Out in Another Classroom.** Send the student to another classroom for approximately twenty minutes with academic work. This is a useful corrective action, especially if you do not have administrative support. Make arrangements with the teacher in the other classroom beforehand.

7. **Immediate Call to Parents.** Calling parents—with the student present—at the next break after the student's misbehavior can be a powerful corrective action. Such immediate action can have a real impact. If necessary, call the parents at work. If your classroom does not have a phone, use your own cell phone.

Corrective Actions Should Be Organized in a Hierarchy

The best way to use corrective actions is to organize them into a hierarchy. A hierarchy lists the corrective actions in the order in which they will be imposed for inappropriate behavior during a day or period.

A hierarchy is progressive and starts with a reminder. Corrective actions in the hierarchy then become gradually more substantial for the second, third, fourth, and fifth times that a student chooses to misbehave.

Sample Hierarchy for Grades K–3

First time: Warning
Second time: Five-minute time out away from other students
Third time: Miss free choice time
Fourth time: Call parents
Fifth time: Send to office

Sample Hierarchy for Grades 4–6

First time: Warning
Second time: Fill out Think Sheet and send to parent
Third time: Miss free choice time
Fourth time: Call parents
Fifth time: Send to office

Sample Hierarchy for Middle/Secondary Classroom

First time: Warning
Second time: Think Sheet
Third time: After-school detention
Fourth time: Send to office

Discipline Hierarchy Should Also Include a Severe Clause

A *severe clause* states that if a student is severely disruptive, for example, defiant, violent, or destroys property, you need to skip all the other steps of the hierarchy and immediately send the student to the administrator's office.

Each Day Students Start Over With a Clean Slate

No matter how far students have gone the previous day on your discipline hierarchy, the next day they should start out fresh. That means the first time they disrupt each day, they would receive a warning. The only exception will be students who are on individualized behavior plans discussed in chapter 15, "Develop Individualized Behavior Plans."

Keep Track of Corrective Actions

For your hierarchy to be simple to use and easy to integrate into your teaching routine, you will need a system to keep track of student misbehavior and the corrective actions accrued each day. You'll need to know at a glance the names of students who have received corrective actions and where they are in the hierarchy. Keeping track doesn't have to be time consuming and it doesn't have to interrupt your teaching. Here are some suggestions:

1. **Write Disruptive Students' Names on a Clipboard.** The first time a student misbehaves, write his or her name on your clipboard. If the student misbehaves again, put a check next to his or her name and continue doing so each time the misbehavior occurs. At a glance you will know how far down on the hierarchy each student has gone and the corrective actions he or she has chosen. Place a blank sheet on the clipboard each morning.

2. **Use a Color-Coded Card System.** As an alternative to recording students' disruptions on a clipboard, some elementary teachers use a color-coded card system. To use this system, you will want to make a chart of students' names with a pocket under each name. In the pocket put five different-colored cards. Each color signifies a different place on the hierarchy.

> Green: No corrective actions   Orange: Third time student misbehaves
> Blue: First time student misbehaves   Red: Fourth time student misbehaves
> Yellow: Second time student misbehaves Purple: Fifth time student misbehaves

At the beginning of the day, all students have a green card showing in the pocket under their name. The first time a student misbehaves, you move the green card to the back of the deck, leaving the blue card showing. This indicates the student has received a reminder.

Each successive time a student misbehaves, the front card goes to the back, exposing the card that indicates where he or she is now on the hierarchy. At the end of the school day, a student helper puts all the cards back in order for the beginning of the next day.

> Word of warning: Always be the one to change the students' cards if they are disruptive. Many teachers have students move their own card and oftentimes this leads to further problems, such as the students will dawdle and take forever to change their card or, if you're not watching, change the card of another student instead.

Before You Implement Your Classroom Management Plan

There are several steps you will want to take to maximize the effectiveness of your classroom management plan.

Teach the Plan to Your Students

The first day of school you will want to teach your students all the aspects of your classroom management plan. Make sure they learn your class rules, what positive support you will provide if they follow the rules, and the disciplinary consequences they will receive if they choose not to. (Details on how to teach such a lesson to students at different grade levels can be found in chapter 7, "Teach Policies and Procedures at the Beginning of the School Year," on page 39.)

Post the Plan in Your Classroom

Make a chart listing your classroom rules, positive incentives, and discipline hierarchy. Place the chart in a prominent place in the classroom so that it is easy for you to refer to as you are teaching your students appropriate behavior at the beginning of the year.

Make Sure Parents and Administrators Are Familiar With Your Plan

In order to help gain the support of your students' parents and your administrator(s), be sure to send them a copy of your classroom management plan at the beginning of the school year.

> ### ▶ Key Points to Remember ◀
>
> Students need the limits that can be provided by your corrective actions.
>
> Carefully plan out what consequences you will utilize.
>
> Make sure the consequences are included in a discipline hierarchy.
>
> Have a system to keep track of the consequences your students have received.
>
> Plan out the steps you will take to maximize the effectiveness of your classroom management plan.

Teach Policies and Procedures at the Beginning of the School Year

CHAPTER 7

The beginning of the school year is filled with "first times" for students in your classroom: first time to enter the classroom, first time to pay attention to your lesson, first time to work independently, first time to pass out and collect papers, first time to get ready to leave class, and so on.

How do you want students to behave the first time they engage in these or any other activities in your classroom? How are you going to teach the students how to do so?

Effective classroom managers have learned the following: the number one topic to teach at the beginning of the year is not the three Rs—reading, writing, and arithmetic—it is teaching the "fourth R": responsible behavior.

Why do effective teachers teach and reteach their behavioral expectations so that every student knows exactly how to handle every single classroom activity or procedure? Just look at the facts.

> Teachers who systematically teach their students classroom policies and procedures at the beginning of the year:
>
> - Reduce disruptive behavior by 28 percent (Marzano, Marzano, & Pickering, 2003)
> - Increase time spent on instruction up to one hour per day (LaFleur, Witt, Naquin, Harwell, & Gilbertson, 1998)

In order to take charge of your classroom, you will need to know how you want your students to behave during each and every classroom activity from the first moment students enter your classroom until the last moment they leave.

Determine Policies and Procedures

Your school day is made up of many specific activities that can be categorized into three basic types.

39

Instructional Activities in Which Students Will Be Learning

Teacher-directed instruction
Whole-class discussion
Sitting on the rug
Independent work
Working with a partner
Teacher working with a small group while other students work
  independently
Working in groups
Taking tests
Working at centers
Working at labs

Procedures and Basic Routines That Involve Movement Into, Within, and Out of the Classroom

Responding to an attention-getting signal
In-seat transitions
Out-of-seat transitions
Lining up to leave the classroom
Walking in line
Entering the classroom after recess, lunch, or the beginning of the period
Going to pull-out programs
Distributing and collecting materials/papers
Attending an assembly
Emergency drills
Beginning-of-the-day or period routine
End-of-the-day or period routine

Policies and Expectations That Are in Effect at All Times in the Classroom

Classroom rules
Positive feedback
Corrective actions
Classroom interruptions
Late or missing assignments
Student helpers
Bringing appropriate materials to class
Making up missed work due to an absence
Sharpening pencils
Using materials on bookshelves or in cabinets
Leaving class to go to the restroom
Taking care of desks, tables, and chairs
Using the drinking fountain

In order to create a classroom environment that promotes academic success, first you must know how you want your students to behave in specific activities and situations. Then you need to plan how you will teach them your behavioral expectations.

Planning to Teach a Lesson on Responsible Behavior

Effective teachers go about teaching their students responsible behavior in the same manner as they would any academic subject (Evertson & Harris, 1997). Although there is no one way to teach appropriate behavior, effective teachers' lessons typically follow a systematic format that addresses the needs of the different learning styles of the students.

> Before teaching any lesson, it is important to do some planning. The same is true for lessons on responsible behavior.

Determine Behaviors to Be Taught

The foundation of any lesson is the behaviors you want the students to learn to ensure their success in the activity. You will teach your students the behaviors you want to see and hear during the specific activity or situation. Here are some guidelines for determining the behaviors you will want to teach.

Teach a Limited Number of Behaviors

For each activity, the number of behaviors to learn should be only three or four. Too many behaviors are hard for students to master.

Behaviors Should Be Observable

Whenever possible, the behaviors should be observable—things you can see and hear—such as keeping your hands to yourself, staying seated, and no talking. Avoid vague directions such as "act appropriately" and "be responsible." The more clear the direction, the higher the probability the students will understand exactly what you want them to do.

Prepare Visual Aids

Just as you use visual aids in presenting academic material, it's often a good idea to do the same when teaching behavior. You may want to list the behaviors being taught on an overhead transparency, flipchart, or PowerPoint® presentation.

Examples of Typical Behaviors Teachers Need for Various Classroom Activities

Attention-Getting Signal

When given a signal, students will:

- "Freeze"
- Look at the teacher
- Silently listen to the teacher

Teacher-Directed Instruction

Students are expected to:

- Follow directions
- Sit up straight and keep their eyes on the teacher
- Do this without talking

During a Whole-Class Discussion

Students are expected to:

- Raise hand and wait to be called on before speaking
- Sit up straight and look at the student who is speaking
- Stay seated

During Independent Work

Students are expected to:

- Do the assigned work
- Stay in their seats
- Not talk
- Select an activity from the to-do list if finished early

Working With a Partner

Students are expected to:

- Sit facing their partner
- Speak in a quiet 12-inch voice
- Work on the assigned activity

Working in Groups

Students are expected to:

- Work on the assignment
- Stay seated
- Talk only about the assignment and in quiet voices

Teacher Working With a Small Group While Other Students Work Independently

When transitioning from their seats to the small group, students will:

- Stand up quietly and push in their chairs
- Bring needed materials (reading book, notebook, chair)

- Walk directly to the small group and take a seat
- Not talk

When working independently at their seats, students will:

- Do the assigned work
- Save questions until the group's transition (use Help Card)
- Stay seated
- Not talk

When participating in small-group instruction, students will:

- Follow directions
- Raise their hands and wait to be called on before speaking
- Stay seated

When transitioning from the small group back to their seats, students will:

- Take their materials and go directly to their seats
- Get right back to work
- Not talk

Working in Labs

Students are expected to:

- Follow all safety procedures
- Stay at assigned station
- Use a 12-inch voice

Beginning of the Day or Period Routine

Students are expected to:

- Put away belongings
- Get right to work
- Not talk

In-Seat Transition

When asked to clear their desks for a new activity, students will:

- Put away materials
- Stay seated
- Not talk

Getting Ready for the Next Activity

When given directions to begin a new activity, students will:

- Take out materials
- Stay seated
- Not talk

Lining Up to Leave the Classroom

When told to get ready to line up, students will:

- Follow directions to get ready to leave

continued on next page →

- Not talk
- Gather materials they will bring to the line (lunch, sports equipment, books)

When told to line up, students will:

- Quietly push in chair and walk to the end of the line
- Stand in a straight line without touching anyone
- Wait to be dismissed from the classroom
- Not talk

Distributing and Collecting Materials and Papers

When materials are passed out, students will:

- Take just enough for themselves
- Pass the rest to the next person in the row or at the table
- Speak in a quiet voice

When papers are collected, students will:

- Place their paper on top of the other papers
- Make sure their paper faces the same direction as the others
- Speak in a quiet voice

Responsible Behavior Lesson Format

When teaching a lesson on responsible behavior, you will want to follow the basic lesson structure you would for any academic topic. How you teach the lesson is dependent upon the grade level of your students.

Teaching Lesson for Grades K–3

With younger students you will want to spend plenty of time teaching your lesson, making sure that all students understand the importance of how to behave in each activity. Be sure to use examples, modeling, and constant checking for understanding to ensure all the students understand your expectations.

Teaching Lesson for Grades 4 and 5

Students in grades 4 and 5 want to understand the reasons behind your behavioral expectations for each activity. Explain why you need the specific behaviors and how they will help the students be more successful in school and possibly other areas of their life.

Teaching Lesson for Grades 6–12

For students in grades 6–12, teach your behavioral expectations in a more matter-of-fact manner. These students will probably have been exposed to such lessons in the past, so you can be brief and to the point. To make the lesson as meaningful as possible, explain how your behavioral expectations relate to the real world they'll soon be entering.

The following is a generic version of how you might present a lesson that you will want to modify depending upon the grade level you teach.

Introduce the Lesson

Students are more motivated to learn the appropriate behavior when they understand the value of why they need to do so.

I have a lot of important information to teach you this year to help you be successful students. When I'm up here teaching, I need you to behave in a manner so that I can teach and everyone can learn. For that reason, I'm going to tell you exactly how I expect you to behave when I'm teaching.

Explain the Behavior

You will want to clearly present the behaviors you expect to see and hear during the activity.

When I'm teaching a lesson, here is what I want to see and hear.

First, I want you to clear your desks of everything but the materials I want you to have, such as a textbook or paper and pencil so you can take notes.

Second, whenever I'm talking, I want you sitting up straight with your eyes on me.

Third, there should be absolutely no reason for you to talk when I'm talking. If you have a question, raise your hand, and if I'm ready to take questions, I will call on you and then you can talk.

Model the Behavior

To ensure students have a clear picture of how you expect them to behave, select a few students to model appropriate behavior.

I'm going to conduct a pretend lesson, and I'm going to pick three of you to model what I want to see and hear from students when I'm teaching a lesson.

Also ask students to model inappropriate behavior.

Now I'm going to select a few of you to model what I don't want to see and hear when I'm teaching a lesson.

Check for Understanding

Make sure to determine if the students all understand what they are expected to do. Here are a few techniques that you may find useful to make sure all your students understand what appropriate behavior is expected.

Ask students to repeat back the behaviors.

Who can tell me one thing I will see or hear you do when I'm teaching a lesson?

Ask students to signal their understanding.

If you understand what to do when I'm teaching a lesson, give me a thumbs up. If you are unsure, give me a thumbs down.

Have Students Practice Behavior

As soon as you teach a lesson and the students understand your behavioral expectations for the activity, it is important that they practice the behavior.

> Like any academic subject, if the students do not practice the newly learned behavioral skill, they may never master it.

As students are learning and applying new behavior, it is critical that you monitor them and give effective feedback on their performance. The Behavior Management Cycle presented in Section Four, "Utilizing the Behavior Management Cycle," will be a useful tool in helping you provide students with feedback on how they are learning to behave in a responsible manner.

▶ Key Points to Remember ◀

At the beginning of the year, teach the fourth R—responsible behavior.

Plan out all the policies and procedures your students will need to learn.

Develop lesson plans for how you will teach appropriate behavior for each class activity.

Teach lessons on responsible behavior in the same manner as you would any academic topic.

Develop a Responsible Behavior Curriculum

You would never think about trying to teach students any academic topic, such as reading, writing, or arithmetic, without a curriculum to guide your efforts. The same is true when it comes to teaching students arguably the most important topic of all: how to behave responsibly in the myriad of activities that encompass a school day or period.

Determine the Order in Which You Will Teach the Content

To begin the process of developing a curriculum unit on responsible behavior, you will want to do the following: think about the first days of school and imagine all of the policies and procedures that students will need to learn to follow in order to establish a positive learning environment (see pages 42–44 for a list of policies and procedures).

Once you have determined the policies and procedures you want to teach your students, you will want to plan the order in which you will teach them. There is no one effective order to follow, but keep the following in mind.

Teach the Behavioral Lesson Immediately Before the First Time the Students Engage in the Activity

For example, just before you ask students to do independent work for the first time, you would teach the corresponding lesson.

Teach Lessons for Teacher-Supervised/Directed Activities Before Teaching Lessons for Student-Directed Activities

At the beginning of the year, structure is very important. You will start off teaching behaviors for activities over which you have the most control.

For example, in instructional settings you should first engage in teacher-directed activities because they provide the most structure. You could then have students work independently, because it is slightly less teacher directed. The last instructional activity you would present would be working at centers, because it is the most student directed.

Sample Responsible Behavior Curriculums

On the following pages you will find sample curriculums. As you look it over you may think, when will I have time to teach anything but behavior? Remember, the bottom line is if the students don't learn how to behave in a responsible, nondisruptive manner throughout the day or period, you will never be able to teach them any academic subject.

These sample curriculums have been designed to assist you in planning one that meets your own needs. To help you focus on the types of lessons that need to be taught, I have grouped the lessons under broad, descriptive topics. Use these as guides for zeroing in on issues that are most important and relevant to you and your teaching situation.*

Elementary-Level Curriculum
Day One

Focus on activities that are of basic importance for you and your students right now. You need to get and hold their attention right away for these basic activities. Teaching your students the behavior you expect during less critical activities, such as how to behave during an assembly, can wait until later.

Topic: Teaching Students to Pay Attention. Students need to learn to give you their attention immediately. They also need to learn to be active listeners whenever you are speaking. Suggested lessons include the following:

- Attention-Getting Signal
- Teacher-Directed Instruction
- Whole-Class Discussion

Topic: Classroom Management Plan. Teaching students your plan for how you will deal with their behavior is an important first-day-of-school responsibility. Suggested lessons include the following:

- Classroom Rules
- Corrective Actions
- Positive Feedback

Topic: Student Comfort and Safety Issues. Students need to have their comfort issues addressed. In addition, you must teach emergency procedures. Suggested lessons include the following:

- Individual Students Leaving Class to Go to the Restroom
- Use of the Drinking Fountain
- Emergency Drills

---

* This curriculum is adapted from Lee Canter's *Classroom Management for Academic Success* (2006).

Topic: Ending the Day and Leaving the Classroom. Students will need to be taught your end-of-the-day procedures and how to leave the classroom. Suggested lessons include the following:

- End-of-the-Day Routine
- Lining Up to Leave the Classroom

Day Two

Now you will begin prioritizing behavioral expectations for other activities. Be sure to review all lessons taught the previous day. Without review there is no reinforcement of learning.

Topic: Introduce Your Beginning-of-the-Day Procedures. The first day usually is too hectic to teach this lesson, but teaching it on the second day is very important. Teach the initial procedures first; more procedures will be added on later days. Suggested lessons include the following:

- Entering the Classroom After Recess or Lunch
- Beginning-of-the-Day Routine
- Sharpening Pencils

Topic: Independent Work. Learning to work independently is a fundamental skill that must be mastered before less teacher-directed instructional settings are attempted. In conjunction with this instructional activity, you may also want to teach procedures that are often related to independent work, such as handling materials and in-seat transitions. Suggested lessons include the following:

- Independent Work
- Distributing and Collecting Materials/Papers
- In-Seat Transitions

Topic: Outdoor Management. The second day may be the first time that students will go to lunch and recess.

Because lunch and recess procedures are almost always based on schoolwide policies, specific lessons for these situations have not been included in this curriculum. However, it is important that students understand the behavioral expectations for these activities. Make sure your students understand your school's policies.

Day Three

Review all lessons taught the previous two days as students engage in the activities again.

Topic: Use of Classroom Space. When students start moving around the room, they need to know your expectations for using different areas of the classroom, including their own desks and yours. Suggested lessons include the following:

- Using Materials on Bookshelves or in Cabinets
- Taking Care of Desks, Tables, and Chairs

Topic: End of the School Day. By the end of the third day, students have enough skills to begin learning to take more responsibility in the classroom. Students should be taught how to complete student helper tasks, take down homework assignments, and get the classroom ready for the next day. A suggested lesson is Student Helpers.

Day Four

Review all of the lessons from the previous days as you repeat the activities. Focus new lessons on key recurring activities not yet covered.

Topic: More Beginning-of-the-Day Procedures. Students should be ready by this point to learn the remainder of the beginning-of-the-day or period procedures. Suggested lessons include the following:

- Bringing Appropriate Materials to Class
- Making Up Missed Work Due to Absence
- Dealing With Late or Missing Assignments
- Dealing With Classroom Interruptions (such as when visitors come to talk with the teacher)

Day Five

By day five, students need a day of review. Instead of teaching any new lessons, spend the day reviewing those you have taught, particularly over the last two days.

Less Structured Instructional Activities

The lessons suggested for the first days of school focus on instructional lessons where there is a high degree of teacher control, for example, teacher-directed instruction and class discussion.

> A major mistake of teachers struggling with classroom management is that they attempt to have the students engage in less-structured instructional activities, such as working in pairs, groups, or students working independently while the teacher is working with a small group, before they have mastered the management skills needed to monitor and control the students' behavior during such challenging situations.

Do not even think of having students engage in any of the following instructional activities until you have no trouble keeping the students on task and nondisruptive in more structured instructional activities.

Topic: Working With a Partner. Working in pairs is the most structured learning activity that involves students working together. Students need to learn how to work with one other student before they are asked to work in a group.

Topic: Working in Cooperative Groups. Cooperative-group activities should be taught only after students have learned how to pay attention, work with a partner, move around the room, and get and use materials. Working in cooperative groups is a highly complex activity. Start slowly, focusing first on transitioning to the group and behaving within the group.

Topic: Students Work Independently While the Teacher Is With a Small Group. This is typically one of the most difficult instructional settings for teachers to monitor and manage student behavior. Again, do not attempt this type of activity until you are able to effectively manage student behavior in more structured activities.

Topic: Working at Learning Centers. This is also a highly difficult activity to monitor and manage student behavior.

Start by instructing them on how to use two simple centers. After the students have mastered going to these centers, add more as appropriate. Make sure you are free to monitor students while they are at the centers.

Middle/Secondary-Level Curriculum

You will note that much of the content of the middle/secondary-level curriculum matches that of the one for elementary level, but there are significant differences.

> Many middle/secondary teachers assume that, because of the age of their students, they should know how to behave in many of the activities presented and thus don't need to be taught how they are expected to behave. This is again a major mistake that will, in all probability, have a negative impact on the learning environment in the classroom.

Day One

Focus on activities that are of basic importance for you and your students right now. You need to get and hold their attention right away for these basic activities. Teaching your students the behavior you expect during less critical activities, such as how to behave during an assembly, can wait until later.

Topic: Teaching Students to Pay Attention. Students need to learn to give you their attention immediately. They also need to learn to be active listeners whenever you are speaking. Suggested lessons include the following:

- Attention-Getting Signal
- Teacher-Directed Instruction
- Whole-Class Discussion

Topic: Classroom Management Plan. Teaching students your plan for how you will deal with their behavior is an important first-day-of-school responsibility. Suggested lessons include the following:

- Classroom Rules
- Corrective Actions
- Positive Feedback

Topic: Student Comfort and Safety Issues. Students need to have their comfort issues addressed. In addition, you must teach emergency procedures. Suggested lessons include the following:

- Leaving Class to Go to the Restroom

- Using the Drinking Fountain

- Emergency Drills

Topic: Ending the Period and Leaving the Classroom. Students will need to be taught your end-of-the-period procedures and how to leave the classroom. A suggested lesson is End-of-the-Period Routine.

Day Two

Now you will begin prioritizing behavioral expectations for other activities. Be sure to review all lessons taught the previous day. Without review, there is no reinforcement of learning.

Topic: Introduce Your Beginning-of-the-Period Procedures. The first day usually is too hectic to teach this lesson, but teaching it on the second day is very important. Teach the initial procedures first; more procedures will be added on later days. Suggested lessons include the following:

- Entering the Classroom

- Beginning-of-the-Period Routine

- Sharpening Pencils

Topic: Independent Work. Learning to work independently is a fundamental skill that must be mastered before less teacher-directed instructional settings are attempted. In conjunction with this instructional activity, you may also want to teach procedures that are often related to independent work, such as handling materials and in-seat transitions. Suggested lessons include the following:

- Independent Work

- Distributing and Collecting Materials/Papers

- In-Seat Transitions

Day Three

Review all lessons taught the previous two days as students engage in the activities again.

Topic: Use of Classroom Space. When students start moving around the room, they need to know your expectations for using different areas of the classroom, including their own desks and yours. Suggested lessons include the following:

- Using Materials on Bookshelves or in Cabinets

- Taking Care of Desks, Tables, and Chairs

Day Four

Review all of the lessons from the previous days as you repeat the activities. Focus new lessons on key recurring activities not yet covered.

Topic: **More Beginning-of-the-Period Procedures.** Students should be ready by this point to learn the remainder of the beginning-of-the-period procedures. Suggested lessons include the following:

- Bringing Appropriate Materials to Class
- Making Up Missed Work Due to Absence
- Dealing With Late or Missing Assignments
- Dealing With Classroom Interruptions (such as when visitors come to talk with the teacher)

Day Five

By day five, students need a day of review. Instead of teaching any new lessons, spend the day reviewing those you have taught, particularly over the last two days.

Less Structured Instructional Activities

The lessons suggested for the first days of school focus on instructional lessons where there is a high degree of teacher control, for example, teacher-directed instruction and class discussion.

> A major mistake of teachers struggling with classroom management is that they attempt to have the students engage in less structured instructional activities, such as working in pairs, groups, or students working independently while the teacher is working with a small group, before they have mastered the management skills needed to monitor and control the students' behavior during such challenging situations.

Do not even think of having students engage in any of the following instructional activities until you have no trouble keeping the students on task and nondisruptive in more structured instructional activities.

Topic: **Working With a Partner.** Working in pairs is the most structured learning activity that involves students working together. Students need to learn how to work with one other student before they are asked to work in a group.

Topic: **Working in Cooperative Groups.** Cooperative group activities should be taught only after students have learned how to pay attention, work with a partner, move around the room, and get and use materials. Working in cooperative groups is a highly complex activity. Start slowly, focusing first on transitioning to the group and behaving within the group.

Topic: **Students Work Independently While the Teacher Is With a Small Group.** This is typically one of the most difficult instructional settings for teachers to monitor and manage student behavior. Again, do not attempt this type of activity until you are able to effectively manage student behavior in more structured activities.

Topic: **Working at Labs.** This is also a highly difficult activity to monitor and manage student behavior. Make sure you are free to monitor students while they are working at their lab activities.

Teaching Responsible Behavior Lesson List

Instructional Settings Lessons

——— Teacher-Directed Instruction

——— Whole-Class Discussion

——— Sitting on the Rug

——— Independent Work

——— Working With a Partner

——— Teacher Working With a Small Group While Other Students Work Independently

——— Working in Groups

——— Taking Tests

——— Working at Centers

——— Working in Labs

Procedures Lessons

——— Attention-Getting Signal

——— In-Seat Transitions

——— Out-of-Seat Transitions

——— Lining Up to Leave the Classroom

——— Walking in Line

——— Entering the Classroom After Recess or Lunch

——— Beginning-of-the-Day or -Period Routine

——— End-of-the-Day or -Period Routine

——— Distributing and Collecting Materials/Papers

——— Attending an Assembly

——— Emergency Drills

Policies Lessons

——— Classroom Rules

——— Positive Feedback

——— Corrective Actions

——— Student Helpers

——— Bringing Appropriate Materials to Class

———Making Up Missed Work Due to Absence

———Sharpening Pencils

———Using Materials on Bookshelves or in Cabinets

———Leaving Class to Go to the Restroom

———Dealing With Classroom Interruptions

———Dealing With Late or Missing Assignments

———Taking Care of Desks, Tables, and Chairs

———Going to Pull-Out Programs

———Using the Drinking Fountain

▶ Key Points to Remember ◀

As with any academic unit, you need to develop a curriculum for how you are going to teach responsible behavior.

Determine the order in which you will teach each lesson.

Teach the students the behavioral lesson immediately before they engage in the activity for the first time.

Effectively Communicate Explicit Directions

CHAPTER 9

You teach your students the policies and procedures for how you expect them to behave at the beginning of the year. Now you face the question of how to ensure they meet these expectations so you can teach and they can learn in a classroom that is free from disruptive behavior.

The answer can be found, as usual, in examining the practices of effective teachers. Great classroom managers teach us that their singular focus at the beginning of the year or when turning around a disruptive class is to motivate students to quickly follow directions, get on task, and stay on task. The fundamental importance of all the students following your directions cannot be underestimated.

> The foundation of managing classroom behavior comes down to your ability to motivate students to simply "follow your directions."

If you give directions to the students, such as "everyone do the problems on page 28 without talking," and some students start talking, while others start playing with their cell phones, do you have behavior problems? That is an obvious yes!

On the other hand, if all the students follow your directions and get right to work on the problems on page 28 without anyone talking, do you have behavior problems? Of course not, and it is that simple.

The Behavior Management Cycle

The question that you're in all probability asking is, how can I motivate all of my students to follow directions and quickly get and stay on task?

We come to one of the key strategies I have identified that master teachers utilize, which is what I call the Behavior Management Cycle.* The cycle is a systematic approach designed to enable you to motivate all your students to quickly follow your directions and thus reduce disruptive behavior and maximize the time available for instruction. This cycle begins whenever you give directions to the students.

---

* The concepts of the Behavior Management Cycle are adapted from Lee Canter's *Classroom Management for Academic Success* (2006).

> **Step One:** Clearly communicate explicit directions you expect the students to follow.
>
> **Step Two:** Utilize behavioral narration to support students who are following your directions.
>
> **Step Three:** Take corrective action with students who are still not complying with the directions.

Step One: Clearly Communicate Explicit Directions

In order to motivate all of your students to follow your directions, you first want to make sure that the directions you give the students are clear and precise—in other words, explicit (Riegler & Baer, 1989). Research indicates that explicit directions are critical to reducing the disruptive behavior of the students (Walker & Walker, 1991).*

Directions Need to Be Explicit

Teachers who are struggling with classroom management issues are often giving unclear or vague directions to their students. Vague directions tell students *what* to do but not exactly *how* you want them to behave to be successful during an activity.

Explicit directions, on the other hand, communicate to students exactly how they are to behave to be successful.

> ## Vague Directions
>
> I need everyone's attention.
> I want everyone to work independently on this assignment.
>
> ## Explicit Directions
>
> I need everyone's attention. That means your eyes are on me, there is nothing in your hand but your pencil, and no one is talking.
>
> I want everyone to work independently on this assignment. That means you will work on the assignment until it is completed. If you have a question, you can put up your Help Card. There is no reason for any talking.

The reality is that when you give vague directions to your students, you leave it up to them to decide how they are going to pay attention or work independently.

The problem is that how the students, especially those who are noncompliant, choose to follow your directions may not be what you want, and disruptive behavior is the result.

---

* In many instances the directions you give the students may be similar or the same as those you presented to the students in the lessons you taught at the beginning of the year discussed in Section Three, "Teaching Responsible Behavior."

How to Determine Explicit Directions for an Activity

Again, explicit directions communicate to the students how you expect them to behave during the upcoming activity. To effectively let students know how they are to behave, you need to let them know what verbal behavior, physical movement, and participation you are looking for (Witt, LaFleur, Naquin, & Gilbertson, 1999).

Verbal Behavior. Far and away the most common disruptive behavior you encounter is some form of inappropriate talking, such as talking when you're talking, talking when they should be working, and talking too loud.

> Studies indicate up to 80 percent of the disruptive behavior in classrooms today is related to students' inappropriate verbal behavior (Jones, 2000).

Whenever you give directions to your students, you need to explicitly know and communicate what verbal behavior is expected.

No talking.
Use your 12-inch voice.
Raise your hand and wait to be called upon before you speak.

Physical Movement. The next most common disruptive behavior involves inappropriate student movement, such as getting up when they should be seated, touching another student, rocking in their chair, tapping their fingers, and so on.

> Inappropriate movement accounts for approximately 15 percent of the disruptive behavior in your class (Jones, 2000).

Thus, the second area in which you need to know and communicate what behavior you expect when you give directions relates to student movement.

Stay in your seat.
Walk.
Go directly to your seat.

Participation in Activity. In most activities you ask students to engage in, you need to know how you want them to participate in the activity in order to be successful. Thus, the third area in which you need to know what behavior you expect is how you want the students to participate in an activity.

Get right to work.
Do your own work.
Take turns with your partner.

Further examples of explicit directions:

I'm going to be reviewing the points we covered yesterday. Again, when I'm up here I expect everyone to show me they are paying attention by having their eyes on me, sitting up in learning position, and there will be no talking until I ask for questions.

It is time to go to your learning groups. When I say "go," I want you to quietly walk directly to your groups, sit down, and get to work using your 12-inch voice.

When you make your directions more explicit you will probably find that many of your students benefit from your added specificity. Many students have various learning issues, and the increased specificity of your directions will make it easier for them to operate more successfully in the classroom.

How to Effectively Communicate Explicit Directions

There are some basic guidelines that effective teachers follow when giving directions to their students (Canter & Canter, 2001a).

Use an Attention-Getting Signal

You need to make sure that all of your students are paying attention whenever you give directions. You will want to utilize an attention-getting signal to ensure everyone is listening to you. Students need to be taught that when you use your signal, they are to stop what they are doing, immediately look at you, and listen to what you are saying.

Effective attention-getting signals include the following:

- Counting down; for example, "three, two, one, and silent"
- Flashing the lights
- Ringing a bell
- Using a hand signal, such as one hand in the air and the other hand with one finger on the lips ("shh" sign)
- Rhythmically clapping; for example, "When you hear me clapping, join in with me. When I stop clapping, you stop clapping, look at me, and listen."

Check for Understanding

With all students, even those at the middle/secondary level, whenever you give directions it is important to check to see if they understand them. It is not uncommon for students you find challenging to have learning issues that make it harder for them to comprehend your directions. There are various strategies you can use to determine if the students understand your directions.

Have students repeat back the directions: call on students (particularly students who have trouble following directions—when appropriate), and have them repeat back to you the behaviors they are expected to engage in during the upcoming activity.

I'm going to call on students and have them tell me one behavior I want to see and hear when I tell you to go back to your seats.

Have students signal understanding: ask the students to indicate if they do or do not understand the directions.

If you understand the directions give me a thumbs up, and if you don't, give me a thumbs down.

Cue the Students to Start the Activity

Often when you give directions to students, they will begin the activity before you are ready for them to do so. Always be sure to tell them:

I do not want anyone to start the activity until I say go.

> ► **Key Points to Remember** ◄
>
> The Behavior Management Cycle is an effective strategy to teach students to follow your directions, get on task, and stay on task.
>
> The first step of the Behavior Management Cycle is to effectively give explicit directions.
>
> Your directions should always include the appropriate verbal behavior, movement, and participation you desire.
>
> When giving directions, always have all the students' attention, check for understanding, and cue the students to start.

Utilize Behavioral Narration

CHAPTER
10

In the first step of the Behavior Management Cycle, you communicate to the students the directions for how they are expected to behave. The next step is to motivate your students to follow your directions.

The Trap of Responding to Off-Task Students

If you're like most teachers, experience has taught you that some of your students simply do not follow the directions you give them. What happens next? In all probability, out of frustration, you immediately focus on students who aren't doing what you want.

Seth, go back to your seat and stop talking.
Cody, stop fooling around and get to work.
Janelle, there is no reason to be talking when I ask for your attention.

Let's look at the unintended consequences of consistently responding to the students who are not following your directions.

First, what kind of tone do you set in a classroom by basically nagging at the students to do what you want? You know it is negative, the students simply do not like it, and it will in no way help you build positive relationships with your students.

Second, what are you teaching the students by constantly focusing on those who do not do what you want? Basically this: if you want to get the teacher's attention, the best way to do so is by not following his or her directions and by being disruptive. Thus, you're inadvertently reinforcing the exact behavior you don't want.

Third, how do you feel after a day of being negative with students? Lousy—you didn't go into teaching to be a nag.

Two questions need to be answered: How can you avoid the trap of simply responding to off-task students? And more important, how can you motivate all your students to quickly follow your directions and get on task?

Behavioral Narration

The answer to both of the aforementioned questions can be found through the use of effective positive feedback.

> Of all the forms of positive feedback I have ever seen teachers utilize, the most effective is what I call *behavioral narration*.

Here is how you can utilize behavioral narration. When you finish giving directions to the students, you immediately monitor the class looking for students who are complying, and then you simply narrate or describe what you see them doing.

> When I say, "go," I want everyone to take out their journal and immediately begin their writing assignment, and I want you to do this without talking. I'll be looking for students who are following my directions. Ready, go!

> Liza is taking her journal out without talking, Kahil has his journal out and has begun writing, and Tyisha got right to work writing in her journal and is not talking.

If you are a middle/secondary teacher working with older students who often don't like being singled out for being good, you will want to narrate groups of students who are following your directions.

> I see table one's students are taking out their journals without talking. Students at table three have already begun silently writing in their journals.

Benefits of Utilizing Behavioral Narration

Why is this such an effective classroom management tool? Let's take a closer look at the benefits you can realize by using behavioral narration in your classroom.

Behavioral Narration Enables You to Repeat Directions in a Positive Manner

When you utilize behavioral narration, you are basically repeating your directions to the students by describing the behavior of those students who are following your directions.

> Direction: *Take out your book and immediately get to work.*
> Behavioral narration: *Kyla has taken out her book and has already gotten to work.*
> Direction: *Go directly back to your seat.*
> Behavioral narration: *Kaleb is going directly back to his seat.*
> Direction: *I want you to do work without talking.*
> Behavioral narration: *Row five is working without talking.*

Some students may have difficulty following your directions if you only give them once. Here is what I mean.

First, some of your students who are noncompliant may have learning issues that can make it more difficult for them to process your directions.

Second, the students may not have been listening when you initially gave the directions, and thus will have trouble following them even if they want to.

It is therefore necessary to repeat your directions to help students successfully follow them. Oftentimes you do, in fact, end up repeating your directions—but as in the previous scenario, you typically end up doing so in a negative manner, such as "Let's get to work. I'm tired of having to tell you time and again what to do. Let's get to work on your assignments, and please stop talking."

> The value of using behavioral narration is that it enables you to consistently repeat your directions in a positive manner. It will enable you to go from nagging students to follow your directions, to encouraging them to do so.

Behavioral Narration Enables You to Motivate Students Without the Drawbacks of Praise

There is often confusion about how behavioral narration differs from praise. Both are tools to motivate students to follow directions, but behavioral narration can prove significantly more useful for the following reasons, as first introduced in chapter 3, "Hold High Expectations."

Praise Is a Judgmental Response to Student Behavior

When you praise students you are making a judgmental statement about their behavior.

I like the way Omar went right to work.

Noel is doing an excellent job working on her project.

Angelica has her book out and is working quietly—that is the way students should act and what I want to see.

Such judgmental statements, by their nature, encourage students to do what you want in order to get your approval, and that is problematic for several reasons (Kohn, 1993; Tauber, 1999).

First, if the goal of your classroom management efforts is to teach students to be self-motivated, the constant use of such judgmental, approval-seeking comments inadvertently can teach students that they are to behave not for their own benefit, but for your acceptance.

Second, some students unfortunately do not care about your approval; in fact, they simply may not want it. You have probably had the experience of praising students for their appropriate behavior only to have them turn around and do exactly what you don't want them to. Praising students can often be counterproductive.

> Behavioral narration is simply descriptive. When you are using behavioral narration, you are just verbalizing what you are observing the students doing:
>
> *Everyone in group three has sat down and is now working on their project without talking.*

Through simply describing what you are seeing and hearing, you are giving positive, nonjudgmental recognition that can serve as a powerful motivator for most students.

Too Much Praise Can Sound Inauthentic

Praising students is a useful strategy to motivate them to do what you want. As the old saying goes, though, it is possible to have too much of a good thing. If you are constantly exclaiming how much you like what the students are doing or what a good job they have done or how proud you are of how they are behaving, eventually several problems will develop.

First, you will find yourself being so syrupy sweet that you probably will not be comfortable with how you sound. Whether you mean it or not, after a while students will not buy you constantly telling them how happy they are making you.

Second, eventually many students will come to see that you basically praise everything students do and thus the value of your comments diminishes dramatically.

Behavioral narration is, again, merely a matter-of-fact description of the students' on-task behavior. Given the matter-of-fact nature of behavioral narration, you will find you can use it consistently without feeling phony. Even more important, students will not likely tire of your positive comments and will continue to be motivated by them.

Behavioral Narration Enables You to Let Your Students Know You Are "On Top" of Their Behavior in a Positive Manner

As a teacher, you need to let your students know that you are "with it" or "on top" of what is going on at all times in the classroom, and are prepared to make sure students are complying with your directions. Why is being with it so important to your efforts?

Your students are always keeping an eye on you and constantly determining if they have to listen to you or if they can choose to do what they want. The more you can convince them that you are on top of what is taking place in the classroom, the more likely they will be to choose to listen to you rather than do what they want.

The reality is that most teachers have been taught that the only way to demonstrate you are on top of students is to be constantly vigilant and immediately respond to off-task students. The issue with this approach, as we have discussed, is that you will find yourself constantly having to be correcting students: "Nickolas, cut that out," and "Let's go, Levi. Pay attention." These responses, again, can set a negative tone in the classroom.

The dilemma you face is this: how do you demonstrate to students you are on top of their behavior without being negative? You come to another major benefit of utilizing behavioral narration.

Immediately after you give directions, actively monitor the students' behavior and narrate some who are on task:

Davis is on his way to his seat, and Annika is working without talking.

By monitoring and narrating behavior, you will send a clear message to all the students that you are aware of what is going on and definitely on top of how they are behaving.

> The consistent use of behavioral narration affords you the opportunity to demonstrate to your students that you are on top of their behavior in a positive manner. This method not only motivates students to follow your directions, but the impact created when badgering stops and positive encouragement begins cannot be underestimated. It can change the entire climate in your classroom!

Utilizing Behavioral Narration to Motivate Students to Get On Task

There are several guidelines to follow to increase your effectiveness in utilizing behavioral narration to get all your students to follow your directions.

Follow the Two-Second Rule to Get Students On Task

Upon giving directions to your students, your number-one priority needs to be to follow the two-second rule.

> ### Two-Second Rule
> Within two seconds of completing any directions, begin narrating the behavior of students who are on task.

Why do you need to immediately monitor the students' behavior and narrate those who are following your directions? If you don't quickly narrate, students will assume you are not on top of what is going on, and they may begin to test your authority.

Describe the Behavior of Two or Three Students

After you give your directions, you will want to describe the behavior of two or three students who are complying (Colvin & Lazar, 1997). There are several benefits to following this guideline: first, you have sufficiently repeated the directions to ensure that all the students understand them, and second, you have let the students know you are aware of how they are behaving.

Use a Strong Teacher Voice When Narrating

As stated earlier, most educators think about using a strong teacher voice only when correcting off-task or disruptive students. It is equally important that you use a firm, strong voice that all students can hear when narrating so you let all students know you are again definitely "with it" and aware of all that is going on in your classroom.

Constantly Monitor and Narrate the Behavior of Difficult Students

When you are monitoring the class to see if students are complying with your directions, be sure to keep an eye on those students who have difficulty following directions to determine if they are on task. This will enable you to accomplish two goals.

First, when you are monitoring students, and especially when you make eye contact, you let them know you are aware of how they are behaving. For most students this will increase the probability that they will do what you want.

Second, if you are monitoring particular students' behavior and they do follow your directions, you will have an opportunity to narrate their behavior, which will further motivate them.

Narrate Before You Correct Student Behavior

Again, don't fall into the negativity trap of responding to off-task students. Resist the temptation to correct their behavior until you have described the behavior of two or three on-task students. This will only take a few seconds and can serve as a positive cue to get the off-task students quickly on task.

Let me be clear: there are obviously exceptions to the idea that you should use behavioral narration before you correct an off-task student.

> If a student's behavior is so disruptive that it interferes with the functioning of the class, such as screaming out or defiance, you will have to immediately correct it.

Use Behavioral Narration as Frequently as Student Behavior Demands

When you begin using behavioral narration at the beginning of the school year or when turning around a disruptive class, use it every time you give your directions. Most teachers find that this simple change in how they manage behavior has a dramatic effect on the classroom.

Over time you can reduce the frequency of using behavioral narration. See chapter 12, "Teach Students to Manage Their Own Behavior," for specific guidelines on how to do so.

Use Behavioral Narration With a Classwide Reward System

Some teachers find that an effective strategy to further increase the impact of positive behavioral feedback is to combine it with a classwide reward system (Marzano, Marzano, & Pickering, 2003). See chapter 5, "Determine Positive Support Strategies," for details on how to develop a classwide reward system.

For example, if you were using a points-on-the-board reward system you might state:

Vic and Jamie are working at their seats without talking. That is a point for the class toward extra free time.

Utilizing Behavioral Narration to Keep Students On Task During Instructional Activities

Behavioral narration is also a valuable strategy to motivate students to stay on task during instructional activities. In combination with effective instructional activities, you will find you can significantly reduce the off-task, disruptive behavior of students.

Follow the One-Minute Rule to Keep Students On Task

Behavioral narration is also a highly effective tool to enable you to deal with another frustrating problem: keeping students on task during instructional activities. Why is this a problem? I'm sure you have experienced the following scenarios.

You start teaching a lesson and have all the students' attention, only to find in a few minutes that some of the students start zoning out or talking, and quickly more and more students follow their lead.

The students start working independently. They are all silent, but as soon as some students start talking, a "low buzz" begins, and in no time it seems like more students are talking and fooling around than working.

> When you have the students engaged in an instructional activity, you need to make managing the students' behavior a top priority (Jones, 2000).

Thus, while you have the students engaged in any instructional activity, you need to make sure you monitor the behavior of the class and narrate the behavior of students who are staying on task as needed.

As a rule of thumb, when you first start teaching students how to stay on task during an instructional activity, you will want to follow the one-minute rule.

> ## One-Minute Rule
> During an instructional activity, at least once a minute, monitor the students' behavior and narrate the behavior of the students who are staying on task.

You are conducting a direct instruction lesson with the class. Every time you finish a point in your lesson, you scan the class and narrate students who are engaged in the lesson:

Will, Josh, and Estavan have their eyes on me, are paying attention, and are not talking.

The students are working independently at their lab stations. As you are walking around the room helping students, you stop and narrate students who are staying on task:

Everyone at the fourth table is working on their lab assignment without talking.

You have a small reading group working with you while the other students are working independently at their seats. As you finish reading with each student, you look up, monitor the class, and narrate students who are staying on task:

Kishan, Grace, and Alana are still staying in their seats and reading without talking.

Through the consistent narration of students who are staying on task, you are (1) providing a clear reminder to the students of what you expect them to be doing, (2) again sending a message that you are on top of the behavior you want, and (3) motivating students in a positive manner to stay on task throughout the lesson.

Behavioral Narration Is No Substitute for Effective Instruction

Behavioral narration is simply one strategy to help you keep students on task during your lessons; in no way am I suggesting it will replace effective instruction. Research is clear that the more you keep your students engaged, for example, provide them with opportunities to respond during your lessons, the less disruptive behavior you will have (Lewis & Sugai, 1999; Sprick, Knight, Reinke, & McKale, 2006). In chapter 13, "Instructional Strategies That Reduce Disruptive Behavior," you will find a detailed discussion of how to effectively provide opportunities to respond.

> ▶ **Key Points to Remember** ◀
>
> Avoid the trap of simply responding to students who do not follow your directions.
>
> Immediately narrate the behavior of two or three students who are following your directions.
>
> Narrate the behavior of on-task students before correcting off-task students.
>
> Constantly monitor and narrate the behavior of difficult students.
>
> Pair behavioral narration with points on the board when appropriate.
>
> During instructional activities, narrate students every sixty seconds.
>
> Behavioral narration is not a substitute for effective instructional strategies during lessons.

Take Corrective Actions

If you're like many teachers, at this point you're thinking, what if I clearly give explicit directions and utilize behavioral narration but I still have students who are off task and/or disruptive? Now we get to the third step of the Behavior Management Cycle, which is how to take corrective actions, such as directive verbal statements or disciplinary consequences.

Guidelines to Take Corrective Actions in Your Classroom

The following are guidelines that effective teachers follow to enable them to successfully motivate students to stop disruptive behavior and get and stay on task.

Follow the Ten- to Twenty-Second Rule

Let's say you give directions to your students and most of them comply, but a few ignore your directions, start talking, and are doing what they want. Guess how many of your students are aware of the fact that some of their classmates are not listening to you? Basically, all of them!

Never forget, especially at the beginning of the school year or when turning around a disruptive classroom, the students are constantly watching to determine if you will or won't quickly correct the students who are not following your directions. If, for whatever reason, they see that you are not responding to the noncompliant students, your students will pick up that you don't mean business and they can choose to misbehave as well (Witt et al., 1999).

> ### Ten- to Twenty-Second Rule
> Within ten to twenty seconds of giving directions, correct the off-task disruptive behavior of students.

Basically, you have a maximum of about ten to twenty seconds from when you finish giving your directions and cue the students to begin following them to correct any off-task or disruptive students. If you wait any longer, as the seconds progress so will the numbers of students who will join the ranks of their off-task classmates. If you wait long enough, you will probably end up trying to deal with a "pack" of off-task, disruptive students (Kounin, 1970).

You may be thinking, how will I have time to use behavioral narration before I correct students in under the ten- to twenty-second time limit? In reality, it will only take you five to ten seconds to narrate the behavior of on-task students, thus you still have enough time to correct those students who still continue to be disruptive.

> When you effectively use the Behavior Management Cycle, you will find that after you give your directions, you will simply do nothing but monitor student compliance. Initially, you will be narrating those students who are following your directions, and then immediately correcting those students who still choose to be off task.

Assertively Restate Directions

As was stated earlier, when you observe students who are not following your directions, you do not want to nag, threaten, or angrily respond. What you want to again do is use your teacher voice and restate exactly how you want the students to behave.

Ethan, the direction was to stay in your seat when you are working. You have chosen to receive a warning.

Connie, you are to be sitting and looking at me without talking. You have chosen to turn your card.

Olivia, you need to do your own work without shouting out. That is the third time I have had to talk to you today, so you have chosen to have your parents called.

When teachers assertively communicate, they basically tell the misbehaving students exactly what they want them to do—in a calm, matter-of-fact manner (Walker, Ramsey, & Gresham, 2004).

Such direct communication of your expectations is the most effective way you can let students know that you are serious about making sure they stop their inappropriate behavior.

Watch Your Nonverbal Communication

In addition to your words, nonverbal communication is equally as important when correcting disruptive students (Jones, 2000). Be sure to turn your body toward and make eye contact with the disruptive student you are addressing. If needed, get in close proximity to the student to add further emphasis to your words. How you deliver your message is just as important as what you say.

Provide Consequences From a Discipline Hierarchy

As was discussed in chapter 6, "Determine Corrective Actions," you will want to have a discipline hierarchy in place to guide your efforts when students are disruptive. Whenever students choose to disrupt, they will be provided the appropriate consequence from your discipline hierarchy.

Consequences Need to Be Provided to Students as a Choice

Effective teachers let the students choose by their behavior whether or not they will receive a disciplinary consequence (Canter & Canter, 2001a).

It is my responsibility to teach you how to behave successfully in this classroom. If you choose to disrupt rather than behave appropriately, you will choose to receive the appropriate consequence.

Why is giving the students the choice of whether or not they receive disciplinary consequences so important?

By letting the students know they will be choosing whether they do or do not receive consequences, you no longer are the bad guy who is giving the students consequences. It is your students who choose their behavior and the consequences that follow.

Kevin, you were talking instead of working. You chose to stay after class.

Brianna, you were out of your seat bothering your classmates. You have chosen to have me call your parents.

Through clearly letting students understand the choice issue, you are sending a clear, distinct message to your students.

- *You* are accountable for your actions.
- *You* are responsible for what does and does not happen to you.
- *You* are in control of your success in this classroom.

Take Corrective Action Every Time Students Are Disruptive

It is a rule of thumb that your students will not perceive that you mean business until they know you will take corrective action. Provide disciplinary consequences each and every time they choose not to follow your directions (Sprick, Garrison, & Howard, 1998).

Beware the Talking Factor

Earlier we discussed the importance of sweating the small stuff in order to demonstrate to students you do have high expectations for their behavior. Of all the small stuff you need to sweat, inappropriate talking is king.

First, remember inappropriate talking is likely the most common behavior problem you will encounter (Jones, 2000). To put this in perspective, just think about how many times a day you find yourself shushing students or exhorting them to quiet down or stop interrupting.

Of equal importance, inappropriate talking is what I call a *cornerstone behavior*. What do I mean by this? Inappropriate talking is almost always the first disruptive behavior students will engage in to test your authority. Students will carefully observe how you do or do not respond when they inappropriately talk out, talk to their neighbor, and talk too loud.

If students see that you are not taking the small stuff of talking seriously enough to respond in a meaningful manner, they will take this as a clear message that they can test you even further. Soon you will find students getting out of their seats when they should be in them, trying to get out of working, and eventually engaging in worse behavior problems.

> You must understand that students don't become defiant, fight, or have tantrums out of the blue. Your students have tested you to see what they can and can't get away with, and the testing starts with talking.

Unless and until you stop students' inappropriate talking, you will never establish a classroom environment in which students recognize that they have to do what you want versus what they want. Everyone loses in that environment.

Monitor Noncompliant Students and Catch Them Being On Task

Another major difference between effective and ineffective classroom managers is how they respond to students after they have corrected their disruptive behavior. Effective teachers make it a priority to find the first opportunity to catch the previously disruptive student on task and narrate his behavior.

You want to be sure to demonstrate to students that you are not simply going to limit their inappropriate behavior, but that you are committed to supporting their appropriate behavior as well.

For example, Lillie is not paying attention and is disrupting students next to her on the rug. You immediately correct her behavior. As the lesson continues, you monitor her behavior, catch her on task, and state, "Lillie has her eyes on me and is paying attention."

How Students Will Test You

When you set limits, the vast majority of your students will quickly stop their disruptive behavior. The issue, though, is your noncompliant students. Rather than stopping their disruptive behavior, they may escalate their behavior to test your resolve (Walker et al., 2004). Here is what you can expect these students to try.

Students Will Continue to Disrupt

You're going to find that you will have some students who continue to disrupt after you take corrective action. Too often in these instances, teachers, out of frustration, keep giving the student consequence after consequence until he or she is ultimately sent out of the room.

When younger students continue to be disruptive after you have corrected them, you may want to take charge of the situation by using the "move in" strategy.

Move In

Walk over and get close to the student. Show your concern that the student's behavior is not helpful for him or her and that you cannot allow it to continue. Let the student know what consequence he or she will receive if the behavior continues. Be sure to let the student know exactly what he or she will choose to have happen if he or she does not comply with your wishes.

During independent work, Daniel is disruptive and the teacher gives him the appropriate consequence from her hierarchy.

Daniel: Oh, c'mon, man. Just get off my case.

The teacher walks over to Daniel's desk, leans down, makes eye contact, and speaks in a caring, yet firm tone.

Teacher: Daniel, you have chosen to receive the next consequence by talking back to me. I'm concerned about how you're behaving. I want to talk about how we can work this out later. But here is your choice: you either stop disrupting or you are in line to choose to have me call your parents. Do you understand?

Daniel: Yeah.

Teacher: I know you can make better choices about your behavior, and I'm going to help you do so.

Many times, simply getting close to students while letting them know in your teacher voice that you are concerned about their behavior and can't let them continue acting inappropriately is all it takes to get them back on track.

Move Out

With middle/secondary students, it may be more appropriate to move out of the classroom to speak to the disruptive student. Removing the audience of peers may increase the effectiveness of your limit-setting efforts.

As with the moving in strategy, you will want to talk to the student in your teacher voice and let him or her know you will not tolerate the disruptive behavior, but that you want to do what you can to help the student make better choices.

Students Will Argue

Some students will attempt to manipulate or argue with you. They have learned that if they get upset and make a scene, many teachers will back down.

Don't Engage

As was discussed earlier, if students attempt to do this when you set limits, you never want to engage or argue with a student. Instead, stand your ground and calmly keep repeating what you want them to do (Walker et al., 2004).

For example, when entering the classroom, Cleo starts bothering other students rather than going to her desk and getting to work. The teacher walks up to her and corrects her behavior.

Teacher: Cleo, the directions were to go to your seat and get to work. That is your warning.

Student: (Getting upset) I didn't do anything wrong. Josh got in my way so I couldn't get to my seat.

Teacher: (Calmly) Cleo, I understand, but I want you to go to your seat and get to work.

Student: (Still upset) But it's not fair that you always are on me.

Teacher: (Calmly) I understand, but I want you to go to your seat and get to work or you will choose to go to time out.

Realizing the teacher will not engage or argue with her, the student goes to her seat and gets to work.

Students Will Become Angry and Defiant

Some students will go all out and provoke angry confrontations with the teacher in an attempt to get their way. In dealing with such students, it is critical that you remain calm, distance yourself from the student's anger, and be prepared to set firm limits.

Use a Paradoxical Response

In this context it means that the more upset the student becomes, the calmer you must be. The calmer you respond, the more likely you will be able to defuse the student's anger.

> Keep in mind that students may be accustomed to teachers getting angry when they are confronted by the students' inappropriate outbursts. When you stay calm, often the students simply will not know how to respond.

Further, when appropriate, you will want to move the student out, away from any audience that will feed the emotional nature of the exchange.

Send the Student to an Administrator

You must consider defiance as a severe disruption that warrants, in most instances, having the student sent to an administrator.

> You must not underestimate the importance of firmly responding and removing defiant students from your class. If you do not do so, you will instantly lose credibility with your students.

Here is an example of how a teacher can effectively deal with an angry, defiant student.

Shelia is texting on her cell phone while she is in her cooperative group. The other students keep asking her to participate, but she angrily refuses and taunts them for doing their work.

Teacher: What's the problem?

Student: We need Shelia's help. She just keeps making fun of us and won't do anything.

Teacher: Shelia, what's going on? Can't you work with your group?

Student: I'm not doing this stupid a-- assignment.

Teacher: I can see you're upset, but I can't allow you to talk that way in class.

Student: I can talk any way I want. I don't have to listen to you.

Teacher: (Calmly) Shelia, please come outside with me. We need to discuss this. I cannot allow you to talk this way to me.

Student: No!

Teacher: Shelia, you have a choice. Either come outside with me, or you will go to the dean's office.

Student: I don't care. Send me.

Teacher: I'm sorry you made that choice. You need to go to the dean now. I want to talk with you later so we can work this out.

> When you calmly stand your ground, you will demonstrate to students that you do mean business.

You cannot stop students from becoming upset or defiant, but you can choose to respond in a manner that does not sidetrack your efforts to effectively manage student behavior.

Students Will Refuse to Leave the Classroom

What do you do if the student refuses to leave your classroom? Trust me, it does no good to stand and argue with the student and keep telling her to leave.

You know that you cannot leave the rest of the students to physically remove a student from your classroom. More important, you must recognize that students know you cannot force them to go to the administrator. Thus, if you choose to stand toe-to-toe with a student and demand he or she leave the classroom, you're in a no-win position.

Have a Backup Plan

You will need to have a backup plan to ensure you can get the assistance you need from fellow staff members to remove defiant or out-of-control students from your classroom (Charles, 1999).

> The reality is that if you don't have a backup plan, you will be very reluctant to stand up to some students out of fear that you will not be able to handle the situation if they get too upset.

Most effective teachers make sure they have a plan that involves notifying the appropriate administrator or security team member to come to the classroom and remove the disruptive student. Back to the previous example:

Shelia: I'm not going to the dean, and you can't make me.

Teacher: You're right I can't. You either go to the dean, or I will contact him and he will take you to his office.

Now you may be thinking, what happens if I can't reach an administrator or he or she does not show up? If this situation arises the most effective response you can make is to acknowledge the obvious and what will happen if the student still chooses not to leave.

Teacher: Shelia, I can't reach the dean, so here are your choices. You either leave right now, or I will escort you there when the class ends in fifteen minutes.

Knowing how to handle students who seriously test your authority is critical to developing your true teacher voice and demonstrating to students you are a teacher who cares about them and deserves their respect.

Students Test Your Authority—Work on Your Relationship

Teachers in general do not like to be tested by noncompliant students. As a result, most teachers tend to emotionally pull away from students who are stressful to deal with. This is a major mistake! Here is what I mean:

A student is defiant, the teacher has to remove him from the room, and the principal suspends him. The next day when the student returns, the teacher, in a stern voice, warns the student, "I'm not going to put up with any more of your nonsense today!"

A fundamental reality of student behavior is as follows:

The more students honestly believe you have their best interests at heart, the less they will challenge your authority.

When students test you, they are sending up a red flag that you need to immediately put some work into building a more positive relationship with them.

If a student is defiant and you have to send him or her to the principal and he or she is suspended, take the opportunity to call the student at home, and rather than lecture him or her, reach out and show you care: "I don't like having to suspend you. What can we do to make tomorrow a more positive experience for you?"

See chapter 14, "Build Positive Relationships With Students," for more suggestions.

▶ Key Points to Remember ◀

If, after narrating, students are still disruptive, you must take corrective action.

Take corrective action immediately.

Assertively restate the directions the student should be following, and, if appropriate, provide a consequence from your discipline hierarchy.

Consistently take corrective action.

Be sure to correct students who are talking inappropriately.

After correcting a student's behavior, look for the first chance to provide him or her with positive feedback on his or her behavior.

When students continue to disrupt, depending upon their age, use the move in or move out strategies.

Never engage with students who attempt to argue with you.

Use a paradoxical response when students get upset.

Have a backup plan to remove highly disruptive students from your room.

When students test your authority, take it as a message that you need to work on your relationship with them.

Teach Students to Manage Their Own Behavior

If you're like most teachers, I seriously doubt you went into your profession because you wanted to spend your day reminding students how to behave and narrating or correcting their behavior. You probably entered the field because you simply wanted to teach.

After presenting the Behavior Management Cycle in workshops, I often hear several related and important questions from participants.

- If I have to put so much time and effort into managing the students' behavior, how will I ever have time to teach?

- If I'm constantly on top of the students, how will they ever learn to manage their own behavior?

Whether or not these questions occurred to you while you've been reading, it is vital that they are addressed. Central to freeing teachers to teach subject matter is teaching students to manage their own behavior (Savage & Savage, 2008; Levin & Shaken-Kaye, 2001).

The Levels of Classroom Management Structure

When you study effective teachers at any grade level, be it elementary, middle, or secondary, you quickly learn that their basic philosophy regarding classroom management can be summed up by the following statement: from structure comes freedom.

> Effective teachers have learned that the more behavioral structure they provide students at the beginning of the year, the more freedom they are able to give them as the year progresses.

The goal of effective teachers' behavioral efforts is to teach the students to manage their own behavior with as little direction from them as possible. In order to help students reach this goal, what you observe is that these teachers utilize three distinct levels of behavioral structure throughout the school year.

- **Level One: Highly Structured—Keeping a Tight Rein.** This level is utilized at the beginning of the school year or when attempting to turn around a disruptive class. Teachers keep a tight rein on the students' behavior. The number-one priority for the teacher is not academic instruction but taking charge of the classroom through the consistent use of the Behavior Management Cycle.

■ **Level Two: Moving Toward Self-Management.** Teachers move to this level when most of their students begin to follow directions, get on task, and stay on task in all classroom activities. As the students demonstrate they have learned to behave appropriately, the teachers begin to loosen the reins regarding how tightly they monitor, narrate, and correct their behavior. Teachers' priority at this level is both teaching academic content while still being vigilant regarding student behavior.

■ **Level Three: Student Self-Management.** Teachers finally move to this level when the overwhelming majority of their students have learned to behave appropriately throughout their time in the classroom. The teachers' priority is simply to teach academic content. Managing student behavior typically consists of occasional narration of appropriate behavior and a simple verbal reminder or stern look when students are off task.

Let's examine in more detail how you can determine the level of classroom management structure that is appropriate for you and your students.

Level One: Highly Structured

Teachers typically stay at the highly structured level for at least two weeks, though this depends on their level of experience (the less experienced you are, the longer you will probably need to stay at this level) and the difficulty of the students' behavior.

Let's examine in detail how you will utilize the Behavior Management Cycle strategies during both instructional activities and transitions when you need to keep a tight rein on student behavior.

Managing Behavior During Instructional Activities

Your top priority is teaching students how to behave during the activity versus teaching the academic content.

Give Explicit Directions and Check for Understanding

Before each activity, go over the directions, and check to ensure student understanding. Make sure to emphasize that there is to be no inappropriate talking during any instructional activity.

Every Minute Monitor and Narrate Students Throughout the Lesson

No matter what the lesson, make it your priority to consistently monitor and narrate student behavior from the beginning to the end of the instructional activity.

Use a Points-on-the-Board Classwide Reward

Using classwide points to increase your ability to motivate your students to learn to behave during these activities is strongly recommended.

Stop Lesson and Correct Disruptive Behavior Utilizing Your Discipline Hierarchy

No matter where in a lesson a student is disruptive, immediately stop the lesson and correct his behavior, especially inappropriate talking.

Managing Behavior During Transitions

Your priority is making sure students learn to quickly go from one activity to another.

Give Explicit Directions and Check for Understanding

Every time you give directions, you want to tell students the explicit behaviors you want to see and hear and check to make sure students understand. It is helpful to set the expectation that students will remain silent to ensure the transitions go as smoothly as possible.

Break Complex Transitions Into Smaller Steps

In order to ensure students learn complex transitions such as lining up, you will want to break such activities into smaller steps.

> First step: Students get ready to line up.
> Second step: Students stand behind their desks.
> Third step: Students are dismissed by tables to line up.
> Monitor and narrate student behavior throughout the transition.

From the beginning until the end of every transition, let the students know you are on top of their behavior by narrating students who are complying with your directions. Don't get distracted by talking to students or simply preparing for the next activity.

Utilize Timed Incentives

In order to motivate students to learn to quickly complete transitions, set up a timed incentive; for example, if all the students complete the transition in less than two minutes, the class earns points toward their classwide reward or extra, preferred activity time at the end of the day.

Consistently Correct Disruptive Behavior by Utilizing Your Discipline Hierarchy

If your behavioral narration does not immediately get a student on task, correct his or her behavior, no matter how minor. Be prepared for students to test you, and stand your ground.

Level Two: Moving Toward Self-Management

You will usually be able to loosen the reins on student behavior initially during structured instructional activities, such as during direct instruction or independent work. You can begin moving students toward self-management when they are able to go through an entire instructional activity without you having to correct the disruptive behavior of any students. When students demonstrate they can handle this, you can move on to loosening up during less structured, and thus harder to manage, classroom transitions.

How long teachers spend moving students toward self-management depends again on their level of experience and the difficulty of the class. Some teachers find they stay at this level for several months after ending the high-structure level; other teachers need to stay at this level until the end of the school year.

Let's examine how teachers manage student behavior at this level.

Managing Behavior During Instruction

Your top priority shifts from teaching behavior to teaching academics.

Continue Giving Explicit Directions

You will continue giving explicit directions, but will only need to check for understanding if giving directions for new or complex activities.

Reduce Frequency of Behavioral Narration

Since you will not need to be so on top of student behavior, you can reduce the frequency of behavioral narration to every two to three minutes during the instructional activity. Focus should be put on narrating students who are still struggling with self-control.

Phase Out Classwide Reward for Behavior

You will want to begin phasing out giving students class points for appropriate behavior and consider having them earn class points for academic performance.

Continue Correcting Inappropriate Behavior by Utilizing Your Discipline Hierarchy

It is still important to take the appropriate corrective action from your discipline hierarchy whenever students are the least bit disruptive during any instructional activity.

Managing Behavior During Transitions

You still want to make sure students learn how to go quickly from one activity to another.

Continue Giving Explicit Directions

Continue giving explicit directions, but you will be able to stop checking for understanding unless you are asking the students to transition in a unique manner, such as the first time going to an assembly. You should still have students remain silent as they transition.

Periodically Utilize Behavioral Narration

Students should not need such close monitoring or as much narration as they move from one activity to another. Focus should be placed on narrating students who are having trouble with self-control.

Continue Correcting Inappropriate Behavior by Utilizing Your Discipline Hierarchy

You will still take the appropriate corrective action from your discipline hierarchy whenever students are disruptive.

Phase Out Timed Incentives

As the students begin to master how to quickly transition, you can begin to phase out the use of timed incentives to motivate them.

Difficult Students

At this point, if you still have students who are consistently disruptive, begin the process of implementing an individualized behavior plan for each student. Such plans will spell out specific positive incentives, disciplinary consequences, and relationship-building strategies to meet the student's needs. See chapter 15, "Develop Individualized Behavior Plans," for details.

Level Three: Student Self-Management

You will reach the self-management level when at least 90 percent of your students follow your directions, and get and stay on task throughout any classroom activity without you constantly monitoring their behavior. At this level, students are expected to monitor and correct their own behavior with little direction from you.

It is important to note that many teachers, due to lack of experience or the difficulty of the composition of the class, are unable to reach this level at any point in the school year.

Let's examine how you will manage student behavior at this level.

Instructional Activities and Transitions

Your only basic focus during instruction is teaching the academic content. During transitions, you provide minimal, if any, direction.

Give Directions That May Be Vague

Once students have learned how to behave during an activity, vague directions may be all that is needed. Simply saying, "Let's get to work" or "Time to get ready to leave" will be sufficient.

Occasionally Monitor and Narrate

All that will be needed is for you to narrate students' behavior, especially that of difficult students, once or twice during the lesson or transition.

Eliminate the Use of the Discipline Hierarchy

Rather than providing consequences from your discipline hierarchy, you will redirect off-task or disruptive students back on task. You will want to consider the following redirecting strategies.

The Look. Stop the lesson, and give a stern look that communicates "get back on task." Give this same look during transitions when students get off task.

Physical Proximity. Move close to the off-task student, or move the student closer to you.

Use the Student's Name in the Lesson. Here is an example:

> I'm sure all of you, including Raquel, will be able to do this problem when I'm finished.

If for any reason students begin to become more disruptive, simply remind them that you will go back to using the discipline hierarchy if their behavior warrants.

Difficult Students

At this point you will want any students who are still having trouble with self-control to have an individualized behavior plan, as discussed in chapter 15.

Recalibrate

There are times during the school year when you may need to recalibrate the level of structure necessary to ensure the students are successful. By *recalibrate*, I mean you will need to go back to the previous level of structure. For example, after winter break if you are at the moving toward self-management level, you will want to tighten the reins and go back to the highly structured level for a few days to provide the students with the extra structure they may need after being gone for several weeks.

Consider recalibrating your management level:

- After any prolonged break, such as winter or spring
- On special days, for example, Halloween or during a field trip
- When a new student who is disruptive enters the class

▶ Key Points to Remember ◀

Effective teachers use various levels of classroom management structure throughout the year.

At the beginning of the year or when turning around a classroom, you need to keep a tight rein on student behavior by utilizing a highly structured level of management.

When the majority of the students begin to learn how to behave, you can loosen the reins and move toward student self-management.

When the overwhelming majority of the students have learned how to behave in all classroom activities, you can allow the students to self-manage their behavior.

When appropriate, you can recalibrate the level of management you utilize with your students.

Instructional Strategies That Reduce Disruptive Behavior

When it comes to managing student behavior, another key concept to always keep in mind is this: the more your students are engaged in your lesson, the less problem behavior you will have.

The reality is that if you talk or lecture for too long, you will lose your students. Rather than pay attention, odds are they will start to disrupt. The name of the game is to give your students constant opportunities to respond during your lessons in order to increase their engagement (Burden, 2000; Lewis & Sugai, 1999; Sprick et al., 2006).

An *opportunity to respond* is any instructional question or statement made by you that is designed to seek a verbal or nonverbal response from one or more of your students.

Let's read the next sentence together.

I want you to all think about the answer to this question.

If you agree with what I just said, thumbs up; if you don't, thumbs down; and if you're not sure, thumbs sideways.

Increasing the opportunities you provide students to be engaged in your lessons is one of the biggest bang for your buck strategies you can utilize to improve student behavior during instructional activities.

How to Provide Opportunities to Respond

There are several guidelines to follow to ensure you effectively provide opportunities to respond.

Provide Opportunities to Respond Frequently in Instruction

Utilizing opportunities to respond to increase your students' engagement begins with your lesson planning. When planning your lessons, determine when and how you will provide students with the chance to be actively engaged throughout your instruction.

Always keep in mind the rule of thumb is that if you go for more than a few minutes, depending on the age of your students, without providing them with an opportunity to be actively engaged in the lesson, you can start to lose students' attention (Harmin & Toth, 2006).

Throughout your lesson, monitor students' attention level. If you see their attention begin to drift, quickly get them back on track with one or more of the following strategies.

Equitably Distribute Opportunities to Respond

Be aware that for the last thirty years research has indicated that teachers engage in unconscious patterns of behavior that often result in some students having more opportunities to respond than others (Kerman, Kimball, & Martin, 1980). Teachers tend to more often call on high-achieving students who are motivated to learn and usually less disruptive. Thus, you will want to plan strategies that will help you to more equitably distribute the opportunities to respond to engage all of your students, especially those who are less motivated.

Teach Students How They Are Expected to Behave When Provided an Opportunity to Respond

As with any other activity in your classroom, begin by quickly teaching students your expectation for how they are to respond when you use the various engagement opportunities presented in the following section.

Opportunity to Respond to Strategies

Here are some examples of the engagement strategies teachers find most useful to help maximize their students' active participation in lessons.

Questions

Asking questions is obviously one of the most common strategies you use to engage your students. When asking questions you need to keep in mind the importance of equitable distribution of opportunities to respond.

Common Mistakes Teachers Make When Asking Questions

When studying teachers it becomes abundantly clear that when they ask questions, you can count on them to only call on a select few students to answer (Di Giulio, 2004). The rest of the students in the classroom are aware of this pattern, and quickly learn that they don't need to pay attention or think of a response because the odds are they will never be called on. Let's look at which students teachers generally tend to call on.

Teachers Call on Students Who Quickly Raise Their Hands. Teachers are often so grateful to get a response from students that they tend to call on the first, second, or third hand that is raised. Thus, students learn if you wait to raise your hand, you won't be called on.

Teachers Call on Males. The research is clear: teachers call on boys twice as often as they do girls (Sadker & Sadker, 1994). This is due to the fact that boys tend to be more aggressive in their hand raising and because teachers often fear boys will get disruptive.

Teachers Call on Students Who Sit in the "Terrific T." Teachers tend to call on students who are sitting in what is known as the "Terrific T" in the class. Imagine the letter *T* with the top being the front row of the class and the body of the letter being the rows up the center. Teachers' attention tends to be drawn to students sitting in the T, thus they call on those students more often.

Teachers Call on High-Achieving Students. Again, for various reasons, teachers more frequently call on high-achieving students (Kerman, Kimball, & Martin, 1980). It may be that they know these students are more likely to give the correct answer. It also may be that the teachers are concerned about embarrassing other students or are afraid students may answer in an inappropriate manner.

Increasing Student Engagement When Asking Questions

The following are strategies you will want to utilize to maximize the engagement of all your students when you ask questions.

Do Not Allow Students to Shout Out Answers. Often you will find that when teachers ask questions, some students will shout out the answers. When this happens, you're allowing a few students to monopolize the opportunities to respond and letting the rest of the students be passive observers. Clearly communicate your expectations:

> *When I ask for answers, I expect everyone will raise their hands and will not speak or make any noise until called on.*

When asking questions, be sure to narrate students who are raising their hand and not shouting out and, if needed, provide consequences to those who continue to shout out.

Have Students Track the Speaker. To increase the engagement of all the students when one student is answering a question, make sure the class "tracks the speaker."

> *When a fellow student is answering a question, I expect everyone will look at the student and silently follow his or her answer.*

You again want to narrate students who are tracking the speaker.

Have Students Speak in a Strong Voice. When students are answering questions, there is no way to keep the rest of the class engaged if they can't hear what their classmate is saying. Teach the students that when they respond, they are to use a strong voice because what they say is important.

In order to ensure your expectations are met, you will want to quickly cue students whose voices are inaudible to their classmates. Use a quick cue such as "strong voice" to indicate you want the student to speak up.

Direct Questions to the Entire Class. Resist the temptation to always direct questions to individual students by saying, for example, "James, what is the answer to the problem?" The second you let the students know they won't be called on, you let them off the hook and lower their engagement.

Throw out questions to the class. Don't let the students know who you will call on—have them all "on the hook" to think about their answer.

I want you to all think about what the answer to this problem is.

I'm going to be looking for someone who can tell me what the theme of this paragraph was.

I want to know if you do or do not agree with my statement and why.

Randomly Call on Students. When calling on students to answer a question, you should decide whom to call on whether or not they indicate they have the answer. You want to teach the students that you will randomly call on students to answer.

When you randomly call on students, you make sure the students you are concerned about understand what is being taught. In addition, you keep the students on their toes because they never know on whom you're going to call. This can increase their motivation to stay engaged in the lesson.

Effective teachers use the strategy of randomly calling on students as follows.

Frequently call on random students. To maximize the engagement of students, you will need to frequently call on students in a random manner. In a quick, matter-of-fact manner, call on students throughout the room. You want the students to learn that at any time you may call on them whether or not they are signaling they have the answer.

Ask for the students' response in a positive, matter-of-fact manner. The purpose of randomly calling on students is to foster positive engagement and a sense of rigor in the classroom, not to discipline off-task students. Thus, your tone with the students must be positive; you must interact with them in a manner that indicates you expect them to answer.

Use Wait Time. One of the most powerful strategies to improve engagement when asking questions is to simply wait a few seconds before calling on a student to answer (Harmin & Toth, 2006). Most teachers tend to wait less than one second before calling on a student, but this does not allow many students enough time to think about their answer and lessens their engagement.

When asking questions, the key is to wait at least three seconds before calling on a student to respond. Whenever you ask a question, just count to yourself "1001 . . . 1002 . . . 1003" before calling on a student.

Ask for More Hands. Encourage more engagement. If only a few students raise their hands, make it clear you expect more hands to be raised.

I'm waiting for more hands.
I want to see at least fifteen hands.

Pull Students' Names From a Jar. To increase student engagement when asking questions, you can also use strategies that will enable you to randomly call on a student. For example, put all the students' names on a piece of paper or popsicle sticks and put them in a jar. Let the students know that you're going to pull a name out of the jar to answer.

Choral Response

A choral response is when the teacher has all the students repeat information aloud in unison. The classic example is when teachers of young students often have the entire class chant the ABCs. Choral work is a strategy that is valuable at any grade level to help students stay engaged and learn new material.

Everyone read the answer on the board.
All together, what's the formula?
Class, what's 7 x 7?

Choral responses are designed to help students memorize content. Many teachers utilize this strategy along with flash cards. You simply hold up a flash card and have the students read the answer in unison.

Teach Students How to Chorally Respond

Again, as with any instructional activity, you will want to teach the students how you expect them to respond when you have them chorally respond.

First, introduce the concept of choral response to students:

I want to make sure you learn as much as you can. Thus, sometimes when I'm teaching I'm going to use what is called a choral response. That means I want you to be a chorus that repeats what I say, gives an answer, or reads some information.

Then tell students how they are to participate when chorally responding:

When I'm going to have the class chorally respond, I will signal you by first saying "all together" and will raise my hand up high like this. When I drop my hand, I want everyone to answer in a loud, enthusiastic voice. A loud voice is not a silly voice or screaming.

Next model how to chorally respond:

Let's practice how you are to chorally respond. When I say all together and drop my hand, I want everyone to say in a loud voice, "We're practicing a choral response."

Then check for understanding:

If you understand how to chorally respond, put your thumb up; if you don't, put your thumb down; and if you're not sure, put your thumb sideways.

Determine How You Will Cue the Students to Respond in Unison

Teachers use various cues to indicate to students it is time to respond chorally in unison:

- Counting—You can count down, for example, "One, two, ready, you…" or "Three, two, one…" Counting has the advantage of giving students time to get ready, and if you want them to use a really loud voice, prepare to speak up.

- Prompt—You can use a simple prompt such as, "All together!" "Everyone!" or "Class!"

- Hand Gesture—Use a nonverbal gesture. For example, have your hand drop from above your shoulder with your finger in a looping motion pointing at the students. The only issue with hand gestures is you need to be sure the students all have their eyes on you to get the cue.

Demand an Energetic Response From Students

For your choral response to be effective, you not only want all the students participating, but you want them to do so in an energetic manner. If you cue the students to respond and their response is halfhearted, you will want to cue the students to pick it up:

Let's try that again. This time I want to really hear all of you answering in a strong voice.

Periodically Use a Rapid-Fire Manner

Choral responses can be a great tool to really pick up the energy of the students when it ebbs. This can be accomplished by a rapid-fire manner of having the students respond. For example, you may quickly hold up flash cards and have the students rapidly, in unison, read what is on each one.

Voting

In this strategy you ask questions students can respond to nonverbally. The questions can relate to students' prior knowledge of new content, a concept just being taught, student opinions, and so on.

How many of you have been on an airplane?
How many of you got the answer x = 15?
How many of you agree with Jose?

In addition, you can use questions to check the students' understanding of what has just been taught.

How many of you understand this concept and are ready to move on?

First, determine how you want the students to vote. There are various strategies you can use to have the students vote:

Thumbs up if you agree, down if you don't, and sideways if you're not sure.
Hands up if you agree, down if you don't.
Stand up if you agree, stay seated if you don't.

Then teach students how to vote on a question by introducing the concept of voting to them:

> *There are going to be times I will want you all to respond to a question without talking. So I'm going to have you vote on a question.*

Then teach the students how to respond when voting:

> *When I cue you to vote, you will give me a thumbs up if you agree with the question I ask, thumbs down if you disagree, and a thumbs sideways if you're not sure.*

Then model how to vote:

> *Let's practice. Do you think voting will be a useful way to keep lessons more interesting? Thumbs up if you agree, down if you don't, and sideways if you're not sure. Ready, everyone vote.*

Then check for understanding:

> *Do you understand how to respond when I say it's time to vote again—thumbs up if yes, down if no, sideways if you're not sure?*

Quick Write

At strategic points in the lesson, have all the students write the answer to a question, a personal reaction, or a summary of the key points just presented. A quick write not only engages the students but also improves their learning.

> *I want everyone to come up with the answer for the problem on the board.*
>
> *I want you to all write down three things you want to learn about climate.*
>
> *I want you to write down what you feel are the most important points I just made regarding the causes of the American Civil War.*

After a fair number of students have finished writing their answers, you will want to get their responses. Since all students have had a chance to not only think about but also write down their responses, you have a higher likelihood of getting more students to respond than you would if you were simply asking for immediate verbal answers.

A quick write is very simple for your students to do and does not require you to systematically teach them how to do the strategy. All you will need to do is give the students the specific directions for what to do.

> *Okay. Now I want everyone to make a prediction for how the story will end and why you think this will occur. You have three minutes to write without talking.*

Pair Share

Having students talk about their ideas is an excellent way to get them involved in the learning process. Another valuable engagement opportunity is to have the students pair up, talk about their ideas, and listen to other points of view. Pair share can be used with various learning situations.

Teach the students how to engage in a pair share. Again, teach the students how you expect them to respond. Start by introducing the concept of sharing pairs:

> *It can add to your learning to talk to a classmate about concepts I present. Thus, I'm going to have you pair up with another student to do specific learning activities.*

Tell the students how you expect them to behave when in a sharing pair:

> *When you're working with a partner, I expect you will face each other and talk only about the assigned task using a 12-inch voice.*

Ask students to model. With younger students, you will want two students to model.

Check for understanding:

> *Does anyone have any questions about how to behave when you're working with a partner?*

Use pair share to engage students in a new topic. Before you begin teaching a new topic, you can have students pair up and discuss what they already know about the topic or what they hope to learn.

> *Today we're going to be talking about the Great Depression. With your partner, share anything you know or think you know about the topic.*

Use pair share to expand knowledge during a lecture. You can increase student engagement periodically during a lecture by having them pair up and discuss their understanding of key points you have presented.

> *I want you to share with your partner if you agree or disagree with the author's last point and why.*

Additional Strategies to Engage Students and Reduce Disruptive Behavior

There are additional strategies that effective teachers have learned to increase their ability to keep students engaged and on task and to reduce the frequency of disruptive behavior:

- Teaching with enthusiasm
- Effectively pacing the lesson
- Actively engaging difficult students in the instructional activity

Teaching With Enthusiasm

There is a critical aspect of instruction that both promotes learning and reduces disruptive behavior that is largely overlooked in teacher training: the importance of teaching with enthusiasm (Tauber & Mester, 2006). Why is this so important?

Consider the old adage, "It is not what you say—it is how you say it that matters." No matter how well you plan out your lesson, if it is delivered in a dull and boring manner, you will quickly lose the students' attention, learning will stop, and disruptions will begin.

Experience and research tell us that the more enthusiastically teachers present their lessons, the more students will pay attention, learning will increase, and off-task behavior will decrease. This applies no matter what the grade level or socioeconomic level of the students (Tauber & Mester, 2006).

When you talk with effective teachers, you find they understand that they are called upon to educate students who are "electronic-stimulus junkies." They recognize that, when conducting a lesson, to engage their students they need to put on a performance that will hold students' limited attention spans. If they do not, then they know they will pay the unpleasant consequences of failing to do so!

But It's Not My Style . . .

When I discuss in workshops the importance of teaching with enthusiasm, I often get responses such as, "That's not my style," "It would be fake for me to teach that way," and so on. If you think of teaching with enthusiasm as being "over the top" and engaging in disingenuous clowning around, you are correct in believing it is not appropriate behavior for your classroom.

But this is not what I mean by teaching with enthusiasm. Rather, teaching with enthusiasm is teaching that allows you to present the true zest and desire you have for your students to learn the content you are presenting. You present content in a manner that increases the likelihood that students will listen to what you have to say rather than disrupt.

To unlock your excitement and zest, use a few expressive and creative tools taken from the world of acting to help you comfortably put on a performance that can catch and hold your students' attention.

How to Teach With Enthusiasm

Lessons from stage or screen actors help to give context to the importance of teaching with enthusiasm. Actors realize that the writer's words alone convey only a part of the intended message for the audience. It takes the actor's verbal skills, gestures, and facial expressions to bring the author's words to life for the audience.

In reality, it is no different for you with your students. Through teaching with enthusiasm, your words come to life and hold your students' attention.

Let's examine what it looks and sounds like to teach with enthusiasm.

Vocal Animation. There is no quicker way for teachers to lose their students' attention and end up with disruptive behavior than to drone on and on in a dull monotone when speaking. The key to speaking in a manner that holds the students' attention is to vary your pace and volume.

Pace. If you consistently speak at a rapid pace or a slow pace, you will lose your students' attention. The key is to constantly vary the pace at which you speak. You can speak quickly when you want to communicate your excitement. Speak slowly to add emphasis to your words. You can pause to add drama to what you are saying.

Volume. Raising and lowering the volume of your voice helps make your presentation interesting and colorful. Speak dramatically louder when students start to drift off or noticeably quieter when you want students to listen intently.

Eye Contact. You can utilize eye contact when you're speaking to hold students' attention. It is difficult for students to zone out or disrupt when you establish and maintain eye contact with them.

You need to maintain eye contact with a student for at least three seconds to make sure she feels you are really looking at her.

Teachers tend to make eye contact with students sitting by them or directly in front of their field of vision. Be aware of this, and be sure to make eye contact with students who are sitting in the back and on the sides of the classroom.

Movement. You can generate more interest and excitement in what you are saying by moving around the room as you speak. Often teachers make the mistake of becoming stuck in one spot, at an overhead projector, or at the board when they speak.

By constantly moving around the room and reflecting enthusiasm through movement, you can increase the students' interest in your lesson. Move around the room in an unpredictable pattern; this prevents students from mentally tuning out because they don't know where you will go next.

Movement can also be used to engage the unmotivated or manage the potentially problem students. These students will find it difficult to zone out or act out when you're standing right next to or in front of them.

Gestures. Gestures are another tool to increase and convey enthusiasm. Using strong hand gestures can get your energy going. Gestures also add emphasis to your words and help keep students interested in what you are saying. Gestures can also demonstrate your recognition for student performance, such as clapping your hands when students have done well or giving a thumbs up or a high five.

Increasing Your Enthusiasm

If you feel it would be useful to achieve a more enthusiastic teaching persona, you need to begin by taking an honest assessment of your current teaching style.

Videotape a Lesson. The most effective means of assessing your current teaching style is to videotape yourself presenting a typical lesson. When watching the video, ask yourself the following question:

If I were a student listening to me, would I be interested in what I'm saying?

As hard as this question may be to answer, it holds the key to motivating or improving your speaking skills. If your analysis suggests you need to increase your enthusiasm, there are steps you might want to take.

Observe an Enthusiastic Teacher. First, observe a teacher who is known as being dynamic and enthusiastic. What do you see and hear her doing differently from you? Go into your classroom and try to model her speaking style.

Get Real-Time Feedback. In the appendix there is a discussion of the merits of getting feedback from a trained coach to increase your classroom skill level, including your ability to speak with enthusiasm.

"Play Act" Being Enthusiastic. Many teachers find it extremely useful to simply role play or play act being more dynamic and enthusiastic during a lesson. Oftentimes, getting out of one's self by play acting can free you up to behave in a manner you're not normally comfortable with.

When you play act teaching with enthusiasm, watch the students' reactions. Most teachers report students' attention increases. Getting this positive feedback from students can motivate you to continue your new behavior and eventually lead you to be more comfortable teaching in a more enthusiastic manner.

Start With Lessons You Are Comfortable Teaching. When trying to increase your enthusiasm, start slowly. It is best to begin trying new behaviors in lessons where you have a high degree of comfort and confidence. Try incorporating the skills previously discussed for a few minutes of the lesson and again observe the students' response.

Effectively Pacing the Lesson

The pace at which you conduct your lessons will impact not only your ability to keep your students engaged, but also the frequency of their disruptive behavior. Teachers who teach at a brisk pace have a higher probability of increasing student learning and reducing off-task behavior (Jones & Jones, 2004).

A brisk pace stimulates students' attention and participation and reduces lulls in instruction that often result in students getting bored and off task. This point assumes that the content of the lesson is at the appropriate level of difficulty for the students and presented in an appropriate manner, since any lesson in which the content is too difficult or presented poorly will be ineffective no matter what the pace.

Pace Busters

There are classic issues—pace busters—that teachers have that slow the pace of lessons to the point where students get bored and off task. Here are a few key examples:

Bird Walking. *Bird walking* is a term that describes when a teacher starts talking about a point that is not related to the topic of the lesson. When teachers bird walk, their off-the-point topics can slow the pace of the lesson and lose the students' attention.

Too Many Examples. When teaching a new concept, teachers often provide too many examples. After the first few examples, students start getting bored.

Too Much Time to Work. Often the teacher will give the students more time to work on a question or problem than the overwhelming majority need. As a result, when the students get done and have nothing to do, they get distracted.

One Student Working on a Problem. Many teachers ask one student to come to the board to work on a problem as the rest of the students simply watch what the student at the board is doing. This often is not engaging enough for many students. They quickly get bored and lose interest.

Watch Students' Reactions to Determine the Effectiveness of the Lesson's Pace

The key to determining the effectiveness of the pace of any lesson is to watch the students. If the students look lost or get agitated, the pace is probably too fast. If the students look bored and disengaged, the likelihood is that the pace is too slow. If the students look engaged and are on task the pace is probably appropriate.

Actively Engaging Difficult Students in the Instructional Activity

Effective teachers recognize that they need to make it a priority to keep students who have difficulty staying on task engaged throughout instructional activities. These teachers use various strategies to keep these students engaged.

Maintain Behavioral Momentum

There is a law of physics that states that an object that is set in motion tends to stay in motion. The same can be said for student behavior in the classroom.

In other words, if you can get a difficult student on task at the beginning of an activity there is a greater likelihood he or she will stay on task throughout the activity. Thus, you always want to keep in mind during any instructional activity to do whatever you can to get the disruptive students on task as soon as possible at the beginning of any activity.

During Direct Instruction. At the beginning of your lesson, provide difficult students the opportunity to respond.

During Independent Work. As soon as students begin an independent assignment, zero in on students who can be disruptive and make sure you give them the assistance they need to get started on the assignment. Make a beeline from one potentially disruptive student to another, and don't be distracted by questions from less-disruptive students. Once you have the potentially disruptive students on task, then help the rest of the class.

During Pair and Group Work. As with independent work activities, make sure you immediately get potentially disruptive pairs or groups focused and on task before you monitor or assist the rest of the students.

Don't Forget to Narrate Students Who Are On Task

Remember the one-minute rule; every sixty seconds, stop instruction and narrate the behavior of students who are on task, especially those who can be difficult.

Utilize Physical Proximity

Your physical presence close to a student is a highly effective tool to keep students on task. During an instructional lesson, be sure you are close to students who have trouble staying on task. Here are some examples of how to use your physical proximity.

During Teacher-Directed Instruction. Many teachers spend a good deal of class time conducting direct instruction to students. If this is the case for you, be sure that students who can be difficult sit in the front, or as close to you as possible, so you can easily stand by them and get them back on task if needed.

Another strategy to utilize is to free yourself from teaching in front of the class. When appropriate, as you teach move around the room and strategically place yourself by students who are getting distracted and off task.

During Independent Work. When students are working independently, effective teachers make it a priority to move around the room and constantly walk toward or stand by students who have a history of difficulty staying on task during such activities.

During Pair or Group Work. During such activities, spend as much time as possible by pairs or groups of students who have the highest probability of difficulty during such activities.

▶ Key Points to Remember ◀

The more students are engaged in your lesson, the fewer behavior problems you will have.

Throughout your lesson, equitably provide all students the opportunity to respond either verbally or nonverbally to increase their engagement.

Vary the engagement strategies you utilize to include the following:

- Questioning
- Choral Response
- Voting
- Quick Write
- Pair Share

There are various strategies that you can utilize to keep students engaged and on task during instructional activities:

- Teach with enthusiasm.
- Effectively pace the lesson.
- Actively engage the difficult students in the instructional activity.

Build Positive Relationships With Students

There is no question that if you, the teacher, want a disruption-free classroom, you need to go out of your way to build positive relationships with all of your students, especially those who are difficult. Ask any teacher who demonstrates a high level of proficiency in motivating students to be successful, and they will validate this point—and so does the literature.

> Establishing positive relationships with students can reduce disruptive behavior by up to 50 percent. A positive relationship with students reduces disruptive behavior at all grade levels (Marzano, Marzano, & Pickering, 2003).

For numerous reasons, too many teachers are not taking the steps needed to convince their students that they are on their side. One recent study sums up the current perceptions of many of our students.

> Forty-eight percent of students report they don't believe teachers care about them (Quaglia, 2008).

Let's examine why so many teachers have such difficulty building the positive relationships with their students that are critical to everyone's success.

The Trust Issue

Many teachers honestly believe their students will recognize that since they are the teacher, they naturally have students' best interests at heart. As a result of this point of view, most teachers believe the students will trust them and positive relationships should quickly develop. This perspective is valid for most of the students, but unfortunately not so for all of them. Let me explain.

Most students arrive in your classroom with a basic foundation of trust in school and teachers in particular. These students come from homes where their parents back the teacher's efforts and encourage the students to behave and succeed in school. In addition, these students have had teachers respond to them in a caring and supportive manner during their time in school.

Experience has therefore taught these students that they can trust you, the teacher, because they have learned that teachers do basically have their best interests at heart. Because they have learned to trust teachers, you can easily build a relationship with them and motivate them to comply with your wishes and directives.

On the other hand, a percentage of students enter your classroom with very different perceptions of school and teachers. Many of these students come from home environments where the parents themselves do not trust educators due to their own unpleasant school experiences.

Most of these students, especially by the time they have reached middle or secondary grades, have also not had positive experiences in school. These students, for various reasons, often find that teachers respond to them in either a frustrated or angry manner and are constantly "on them" about their behavioral or academic shortcomings. Due to these students' life experiences, there is no way you could say they enter your classroom with the belief that you, the teacher, are someone who they should instinctively trust.

The Unintended Consequences of Assuming You Have the Trust of All Your Students

There is a serious downside to simply assuming your students trust you and your intentions. Basically, any relationship is a two-way street. The students have needs they want you to meet, and the same applies for you.

As a teacher I'm sure you are aware of all that you give to students to help them be successful, such as your time, attention, and knowledge. My question is, have you thought about what you need your students to give to you in order for you to be successful?

Without question, you cannot do your job unless and until your students choose to give you their attention and cooperation.

> Try getting students in their seats and ready to learn if they choose not to listen to you.
>
> Try teaching a lesson if students choose not to pay attention.

Never forget that each and every day in your classroom, the students are making choices as to how they will behave that directly impact your effectiveness as their teacher. When all is said and done, you cannot overlook this fundamental truth of motivating students' behavior.

> The more students trust you and believe you truly have their best interests at heart, the greater the chance that they will listen to you and do what you want.

If you simply assume that all the students have a high enough level of trust, and that they will be naturally motivated to do what you ask, you are, in all probability, going to be sadly disappointed. You will find you have students who are going to continually fight you and give you a hard time by being disruptive and defiant, because in their eyes, you are the teacher, and teachers truly don't care about their well-being.

In order to begin the process of reaching students who have a "trust deficit," it is important to always keep in mind that the deficit influences all of their perceptions and actions. Given this underlying mistrust of teachers, it is foolhardy to expect that these students will be as motivated as their classmates to please you and be compliant in respecting your requests or demands.

Reaching the students whose trust deficit impacts how they perceive and relate to you will take concerted action on your part. The steps you take to build relationships with your other students will be insufficient with these students. You are going to have to convince them that you are on their side, that you are not like other teachers, and that you will ensure they have a positive, growth-producing experience in your classroom.

Steps to Earn the Trust of All Your Students

How can you begin the essential task of building positive relationships with all of your students, especially those who have varying degrees of mistrust of teachers?

To guide you through this process, I want to share with you an activity that teachers in my workshops and readers of my previous books report is highly useful (Canter, 2006).

I want you to think back to a K–12 teacher who you feel was the best teacher you ever had. He or she may have inspired you or even made a difference in your life.

When you think about this teacher, ask yourself this question: what was so unique about how that teacher related to you that enabled him or her to make such an impact on you?

What answers come to you in response to the question? Most teachers come up with qualities such as the following:

- "My teacher really cared about me as a person, not just a student."
- "My teacher was a real person, not just a teacher."
- "My teacher was always encouraging me and giving me positive support."
- "My teacher had high standards and would tolerate no misbehavior."
- "My teacher pushed me further than I ever thought I could go."

The unique qualities that those teachers demonstrated can serve as guideposts for your efforts. If you respond to your students as that teacher did to you, there is no reason you can't have the same impact on your students, no matter what level of trust they bring with them through your classroom door.

Let's break down the steps you can take to build positive relationships with all your students. Please note that some of these qualities relate to concepts presented in earlier chapters, but it is useful to examine how they contribute to building productive relationships with your students.

Establish a Mutually Respectful Relationship

When you ask teachers what steps they think they will need to take to build positive relationships with their students, what you typically hear is "be kind and caring" or "give them praise and spend time with them." There is no question that all of these responses are useful and necessary.

From studying effective teachers, though, I've found that there is an often unrecognized step that must come first to lay the foundation upon which a trusting teacher–student relationship can be built. That is mutual respect.

Students must know that in each and every interaction you will treat them with respect. You must demonstrate through your words and actions that you are someone who can be counted on not to put students down, embarrass, or "dis" on them at any time.

On the other hand, in order to build the kind of relationships you want with your students, you must earn their respect. The reality one learns from interviewing effective teachers is this:

> Unless and until the students respect you, they will not value your praise, positive attention, or extra efforts you make to reach out to them.

As was discussed earlier, a critical component of earning the students' respect begins with you "taking charge" in the classroom. Again, why?

A basic need of students is to know that you care enough about them to take whatever steps are needed to ensure they will learn to behave in a manner that is in their best interests (Brophy & Evertson, 1976). The only way you will be able to meet this need is by taking charge of the classroom in a firm, fair way and standing your ground in a manner that respects the dignity of each student (Canter & Canter, 1992).

So to summarize, a mutually respectful relationship is the cornerstone of your efforts at building positive relationships with all of your students.

Learn About Your Students

Effective teachers understand they are not simply teaching reading, writing, and arithmetic to a class of twenty to forty students. They recognize they are teaching a group of young people who come into the classroom with their own personal issues. These teachers know that if they want to build trust with students, they need to let them know they are interested in their personal interests, concerns, and issues—not just those related to academic content (Smith, 2004).

Student Questionnaire

A "getting to know you" questionnaire is a staple in the toolkit effective teachers utilize to get to know their students (Canter & Canter, 1992). Typical questions teachers find useful include the following:

- What adults do you live with?
- Do you have any brothers or sisters? How old are they?
- Who are your best friends?
- What do you like to do best at home?
- Do you have any favorite hobbies?
- What is your favorite video game?
- If you had one wish, what would it be?
- School would be better if . . . ?
- What did your teacher do last year that you liked best?
- What did your teacher do last year that you liked least?

Teachers who use the student questionnaire report that it enables them to begin to get a clear picture of their students' likes, dislikes, and potential issues they may have. The key point is that these teachers consistently use this information as a guide to building positive relationships with their students.

Student Journals

Another tool teachers find useful with older students is to have them keep a journal of information about their life they are willing to share with you. The information that you glean from the students can prove invaluable. In addition, most teachers comment on what they read. Such comments give you the opportunity to demonstrate your understanding and caring for the issues your students may face.

Provide Positive Attention

If you go into an effective teacher's classroom, you cannot help but be struck by what a positive tone is set. These teachers make it their business to ensure they provide positive attention to all the students each and every day or period. They follow this rule of thumb:

> Make three positive comments to students for each negative one that is made (Colvin & Lazar, 1997).

Providing positive support is especially important in building relationships with noncompliant students. In general, these students are used to getting little or no attention and support from teachers. Teachers tend to ignore noncompliant students when they behave appropriately and respond to them only when they are disruptive (Kerman et al., 1980).

Be Authentic

The teachers who are able to get through to their students relate to them in what would be described as an "authentic" manner. These teachers believe it is important to be a "real" person with the students, not simply come across as "the teacher."

> Effective teachers do not try to be *friends* with students, but make it a goal to be *friendly*.

Let the Students Get to Know You

To be real means letting the students get to know you as a person, not just as a teacher (Smith, 2004). That does not mean sharing all your personal problems with your students, but it does mean letting them know about aspects of who you are outside of the classroom:

- Why you became a teacher
- What kind of school experiences you had, both positive and negative
- If you are married or have a boyfriend or girlfriend
- If you have children or pets
- Your favorite hobbies
- Your favorite music, movies, video games, and so on

In addition, when appropriate, let the students know what is going on in your life: what you did over the weekend or on your vacation, and what's up with the significant people in your life. You don't need to give too much information, just enough to let the students know you are a lot like them and may enjoy some of the same things they do.

Admit Your Mistakes

An important aspect of being authentic is to be willing to admit your mistakes. Don't try to pretend to be perfect. Don't be afraid to admit you've messed up, because the students will lose respect for you.

> Students are not blind; they see when you make a mistake or do not handle situations in the best manner. Thus, if you get upset and lose it, mess up a lesson, or treat students rudely in front of their peers, don't make excuses; sit the class down and apologize.

Students respect teachers who are able to take responsibility for their actions and admit when they have been wrong.

Reach Out

If you want to earn the trust of all of your students, especially those who are non-compliant and difficult, you are going to need to find ways to reach out and let them know you care. Effective teachers are masters at finding the right words or actions that convince even the most skeptical student that they, the teacher, are on their side.

Another way to conceptualize what effective teachers do is to draw from the business world. Savvy businessmen believe that a key to winning over a customer and keeping them happy is to exceed their expectations, be it for service or quality.

Most students who don't trust teachers, again often due to their past experiences, have very low expectations for how teachers will relate to them. They think teachers really don't care about them and will not go out of their way to help them.

> If you want to "win over" students, get them working with you and not against you; you need to exceed their expectations for how they believe teachers will treat them through your words and actions.

Here are some strategies to consider.

Contact Students Before School Begins

Effective teachers start reaching out often even before the school year begins. When they get their class list and identify students who they know have had problems in the past, they proactively reach out to the students by contacting them and establishing a caring tone from the get go.

> *Hi Devon, this is Ms. Levine. I'm going to be your teacher this year. The reason I'm calling is that I want to let you know I'm looking forward to having you in my classroom, and I want to know what I can do to make this the best school year you have ever had.*

In addition to speaking with the student, speak with a parent, if possible, and let them know your commitment to their child's success. Students who have had negative school experiences do not expect to hear from their teacher before school begins, nor do their parents. Many teachers find reaching out in this manner before the students even enter the classroom can help to get the relationships off on a positive note (Canter & Canter, 2001a).

Greet Students at the Door

Here is one of the best opportunities you have each day to show students you care. Make it a point to personally greet and find something special to say to each student, especially those with whom you need to work on your relationship.

> When greeting students at the door, try using the "4-H strategy." Choose one of four greetings: hello, how are you, handshake, or high five (Mendler & Curwin, 1999).

Talk With Students About Nonacademic Topics

If you want to build a strong relationship with students, there is no substitute for simply spending time talking with them about their interests, concerns, joys, and fears

(Good & Brophy, 2003). Students who have troubled relationships with teachers rarely, if ever, have had teachers who took the time to sit down and just be there for them.

> The more time you spend talking with students about nonacademic topics, the higher the probability that you will build a trusting relationship with them.

Contact Students After a Difficult Day

Obviously the students with whom you have difficulty connecting often have rough days that are stressful for you and for them. There is no way the students we are discussing would expect to hear from their teacher in a caring manner after such a day. Exceed their expectations. Go out of your way and make a quick phone call to them before the next school day begins:

Teacher: Jordan, I wanted to touch base about how difficult today was for you.

Student: Yeah.

Teacher: I'm concerned about how upset you were, and I want to see what we can do differently tomorrow so that it is a better day for you and you won't choose to go to the office.

Student: I don't know.

Teacher: It seems you start misbehaving when you are doing work on your own.

Student: I don't like the work, it's boring, and sometimes I don't understand it.

Teacher: Let's try this. If the work is boring or you don't understand it, rather than talking to the other students and getting out of your seat, turn over your Help Card, and I'll come right over to help you. I'd much rather help you than have to send you to the principal again.

Student: I guess so.

Teacher: So what are you going to do if you are bored and need help?

Student: I'll turn over my Help Card rather than mess around.

Teacher: Sounds good. I'm sure tomorrow will be a better day. Have a good night.

Teachers often report that reaching out to students after a difficult day can go a long way in changing how these students perceive them and their intentions (Canter & Canter, 2001a).

Recognize Absences

How do you show your concern when you hear someone you care about is ill? You pick up the phone and call or send a quick email.

Students who feel teachers don't care often believe they are unnoticed in class. When students are absent, phone or email to let the students know they were missed and you care about how they are doing (Mendler, 2001).

Attend Students' Extracurricular Events

Another dramatic step you can take to reach out to your students is to attend events the students are participating in, such as athletic events and artistic performances (Smith, 2004). Difficult students do not expect that their teachers care enough about them to go out of their way in this manner.

> It is hard to imagine a student giving a teacher a hard time or getting in his or her face after he or she has taken the time to attend the student's athletic or artistic performance.

Make Reaching Out a Priority

When I present these concepts to teachers, I constantly hear their concerns about how will they ever find the time necessary to utilize the strategies just presented. This is because they feel they need to put as much time as possible into planning their curriculum and lesson plans. This is a serious misperception. You can't afford not to put in the time to build and sustain relationships.

> Always keep in mind that students who like their teacher are much less likely to take up valuable class time engaging in disruptive behavior.

Further, students who are generally unmotivated by school are much more likely to be motivated to learn if they respect you and feel you genuinely care about their success.

Sometimes the best use of your time to raise the achievement of students is to put some extra effort into demonstrating your care and concern.

Problem Solve With Students

As was just mentioned, to build trusting relationships with students you must be able to communicate with them in a respectful manner. This is of particular importance when you are dealing with continuously disruptive students.

As soon as effective teachers pick up that a student is having trouble learning how to behave appropriately, they sit down with them and have a problem-solving conference. The goal of the conference is not to be punitive, but to gain insight into the student's behavior and, in a caring manner, guide the student to choose more responsible behavior.

The following are the basic concepts teachers use when conferencing with students to achieve the aforementioned outcomes.

Meet With the Student When You Can Give Him or Her Your Undivided Attention

You only want to conduct a problem-solving conference with a student when you can be alone. You do not want to meet during class when other students will be aware of what is taking place or when you may be distracted.

Show Empathy and Concern

When problem solving with students, let them know you are concerned about their success and are meeting with them to help them, not punish them.

I want to talk with you because I'm concerned about how you're behaving in class and want to find out what we can do to work together to help you be more successful in class.

Question the Student to Find Out Why There Is a Problem

Don't assume you know why the student is misbehaving. Do some gentle inquiring about his or her behavior.

Is there something going on that I should know about that's affecting your behavior?

Are there other students who are bothering you?

Is there something going on at home that I should know about?

Determine What You Can Do to Help

What can you, as a concerned teacher, do to help the student solve the problem? You may discover a simple answer that will get the student on track. For example:

- If a student is having trouble in class with another student, tell him you'll move his seat to make it easier for him to control his behavior.

- If a disruptive student is seated in the back of the class, let her know you'll move her seat forward where you'll be closer to help her.

- If the student is disruptive because he or she is frustrated with the academic work, let him or her know you'll provide additional tutoring or arrange for someone else to give him or her the needed assistance.

If you feel that any of these suggestions, or others of your own, may help the situation, discuss them with the student.

Determine How the Student Can Improve Behavior

You also need to focus on how the student can behave differently in the future:

I understand that you're having trouble getting along with some of the boys, but I can't allow you to cuss and yell at them in class. Let's talk about other ways you could deal with these students. What do you think you can do, rather than get so upset?

Some students may not be willing or able to share their feelings about choosing different behavior. If this is the case, help them by pointing out the appropriate behavior. Don't react angrily or irritably to their inability to respond.

Agree on a Course of Action

Combine your input with the student's input and agree on what both of you can do to improve the situation.

I know that it's hard to keep from getting angry with the other kids sometimes. I think your idea of coming up and telling me when you're upset rather than yelling at the other students is an excellent idea.

In addition, I think it would help if each day that you don't get upset in class, I send a note home to your parents telling them what a good day you had.

Restate Your Expectations

Let the student know that you cannot allow him to continue his inappropriate behavior.

I'm here to help you with your problem with the other students. I know you can behave in class. But if you choose to get upset and disrupt the class, you will choose to go to the office.

Summarize the Conference

Wrap up the conference by summarizing what was said. Most important, end your meeting with a note of confidence.

Let's review what we've talked about. When the other students bother you, you're going to come and tell me. If you choose to behave, I'll send a note home to your parents. If you choose to get upset, you'll go to the office. I know you can do better and tomorrow is a new day.

> ### ▶ Key Points to Remember ◀
>
> Establishing positive relationships with students is critical to establishing a disruption-free classroom environment.
>
> You have to earn the trust of many students.
>
> You need to establish mutually respectful relationships with your students.
>
> Learn about your students' lives and interests.
>
> Consistently provide positive attention to students.
>
> Be authentic in your interactions with students.
>
> Reach out and exceed your students' expectations.
>
> Problem solve with students who are having difficulties in class.

Develop Individualized Behavior Plans

Establishing positive relationships using the strategies of the Behavior Management Cycle and following your general classroom management plan can go a long way to helping you motivate most students to improve their behavior. In some cases, however, these efforts may not be sufficient.

With a few students you may need to develop and utilize an individualized behavior plan. Such plans will include:

- The specific behaviors in which you expect the student to engage
- Disciplinary consequences that will be more meaningful to the student if he chooses to engage in inappropriate behavior
- Positive consequences that will be more motivating if he chooses to behave appropriately
- Relationship-building strategies to increase the student's trust

An *individualized behavior plan* is basically a structured intervention designed to give students the attention and support they need to be more successful in your classroom.

Guidelines to Developing an Individualized Behavior Plan

The following are guidelines to use in developing an effective individualized behavior plan.

Determine the Behavior(s) You Expect From the Student

Select only one or two behaviors to work on at a time. Choose those you believe are most important to the student's success, such as no inappropriate talking, no teasing or fighting, or completing all assignments.

Determine More Meaningful Disciplinary Consequences

Noncompliant students often do not respond to the basic disciplinary consequences used in your discipline hierarchy. A warning, time out, or a few minutes after class may not be sufficient to motivate the student to choose to behave responsibly.

With some students, you will find that they reach the same consequence on the hierarchy each day. For example, the student may consistently go to the third step on your hierarchy each day.

> First disruption: Warning
> Second disruption: Lunch detention
> **Third disruption: Contact parents**
> Fourth disruption: Send to principal

This student is telling you that he does not care about your warning or lunch detention, but since the student always stops short of having his parents contacted, you can assume this is a consequence that is meaningful to him. Thus, in an individualized plan, instead of using the ineffective consequences, the "contacting the parents" step would be the initial consequence.

> First disruption: Contact parents
> Second disruption: Send to principal

It may also be appropriate with some students to provide consequences that are not on your discipline hierarchy, such as those that follow.

Have the Student's Parent Come to Class

Few older students would want their parent to come and sit by them in class and monitor their behavior.

Record the Student

Record the student in class, and play the video for the student's parents and the administrator. Obviously, some students will shape up if they know they are being taped—but that's your goal, isn't it?

Plan How You Will Increase Positive Recognition

A natural inclination when dealing with difficult students is to think you simply need to come down hard on them. This is a shortsighted approach because it is important to balance your stronger consequences with increased positive support.

Verbal Feedback

Increased positive recognition begins with verbal feedback. You will want to be sure to utilize the 3:1 ratio of positive comments to corrective comments we discussed before. That means for every statement you have to make to the student about improving his behavior, you need to find at least three opportunities to narrate his appropriate behavior or find other opportunities to praise him for other positive actions.

> For an individualized behavior plan to work, you must make it a priority to find each and every opportunity to provide positive feedback to the student.

Additional Incentives

You may want to consider backing up your positive verbal feedback with other forms of positive support in an individualized behavior plan. What other positive incentives can you utilize to motivate the student? Would he or she like to earn a positive note or phone call home, a special privilege such as being a class monitor, or a no-homework pass? Ask the student what he or she would like to earn.

Make Sure It Is Easy for the Student to Earn the Positive Incentive

Often teachers make it too hard for students to earn any positive incentive, and thus they have no impact on the students' behavior. Make sure students can earn the incentive quickly. The younger the students, the more quickly they will need to earn the incentive for it to be meaningful.

> *Every fifteen minutes that you follow all the directions, you will earn a sticker. When you get twenty stickers, you will earn the right to be my helper.*

> *Every hour you work and do not talk inappropriately, you will earn a point. When you have six points, you will earn extra computer time.*

> *Each period you do all your work and do not talk out or disrupt, you will earn a point. When you have five points, you will earn a no-homework pass.*

Determine How You Will Work on Your Relationship With the Student

Always keep in mind that if you reach the point where you need to develop an individualized behavior plan, your relationship with the student can use some additional work. Should you plan to be sure to greet the student each day when he or she enters class, spend more one-on-one time talking, or maybe attend the student's extracurricular events or even make a home visit?

Some teachers of younger students find that relationship-building steps can be used as positive incentives the students want to earn. For example, if students improve their behavior, they will earn the right to eat lunch with the teacher, stay after class and help the teacher, and so on.

A sample individualized behavior plan appears in the feature box on page 118.

Present the Individualized Behavior Plan to the Student

Meet with the student in a one-on-one conference. Be firm, yet empathetic and caring. Let the student know that you are on his or her side and that you are not there to punish. Make sure the student understands that you developed the plan because you cannot allow him or her to behave inappropriately.

> *Darin, I'm meeting with you because I'm concerned about the poor choices you are making in class regarding your behavior. For your sake and the rest of the class, I can't let it continue.*

Sample Individualized Behavior Plan

Student Name: Darin Marcus

Expected Behaviors

Here are the behaviors I expect:

- Follow my directions.
- Do not talk without permission.
- Complete all class work.

Positive Recognition

- I will let you know whenever I see you following my directions.
- Every hour you behave appropriately, you will earn a point on your desk chart.
- When you have earned ten points, I will make a positive call to your parents.

Corrective Actions

If you choose to misbehave:

- The first time you will be sent to Ms. Tyler's classroom to do your work.
- The second time you will immediately call your parents.
- The third time you will be sent to the principal.

Relationship Building

I will set aside time each week for us to talk about how things are going in school and at home.

It is clear that our classroom behavior plan is not helping you to learn to behave as I know you can. So, I have come up with a special plan just for you to help you be more successful in class.

You will see the plan has special rewards you can earn if you choose to behave, as well as special consequences you will get if you choose not to behave.

I'm sure this plan will help you do better in class and I'm prepared to use the plan as long as we need to, to help you. Let's discuss the plan now . . .

▶ Key Points to Remember ◀

When basic classroom management efforts are not effective with a student, consider utilizing an individualized behavior plan.

The plan should focus on only a few key behaviors the student needs to improve.

The plan should include more meaningful consequences if the student chooses to disrupt.

The plan should include additional positive incentives to motivate the student to choose to improve his or her behavior.

The plan should include strategies to enable you to build upon your relationship with the student.

You Can't Do It on Your Own: Getting the Support You Need to Deal With Difficult Students

A surprising difference I've found between successful classroom managers and those who struggle is the fact that the better the teacher is at management, the greater the probability that he or she will seek the assistance of parents and administrators with difficult students. Why is this so?

The Myth of the Good Teacher

Today most teachers are still burdened by what I call the "myth of the good teacher." This myth holds that a good teacher should be able to handle all behavior problems on his or her own and within the confines of the classroom. The assumption is if you are competent, you will never need to go to your administrator or the student's parents for assistance.

Let me elaborate; do any of these statements sound familiar?

> I'm not comfortable sending students to the office when they continue to disrupt.
> I feel like I'm inadequate when I have to call parents about their child's behavior.
> I think it's my job to handle behavior problems in my classroom.

Did you agree with any of those statements? If so, you buy into the myth to some degree. I cannot emphasize strongly enough that you need to deal with the reality of today's classroom; there is simply no way you can bring out the best in all of your students unless and until you enlist and receive the maximum support possible from your students' parents and your administrators.

> It is not a sign of weakness or incompetence that you reach out to parents and/or administrators for support to help you motivate students to behave appropriately or achieve their maximum academic potential. It is, in fact, a sign of strength: a sign that you are committed to students learning to behave and achieve, and that you will do whatever it takes to ensure this goal is reached.

As I have been writing for years, the myth of the good teacher is nonsense (Canter & Canter, 1976). For the sake of your students and your professional sanity, give it up and look at the steps you can take to get the support you need and deserve in your efforts with your students.

Initial Steps to Obtain Support From Parents and Administrators

There are several proactive steps teachers can take to increase the probability that they will get the support they need from both parents and administrators.

Share Your Classroom Management Plan With Parents and Administrators

Parents and administrators can't support your behavior management efforts if they don't know what your classroom management plan entails. Thus, after you develop your classroom management plan, make sure parents and administrators receive a copy.

Send Parents a Copy of Your Classroom Management Plan

Let parents know how you will be handling their children's behavior. Let them know you have a systematic plan to help ensure their children's success (Wong & Wong, 1998). See the sample Classroom Management Plan Letter to Parents on page 121.

Give Your Administrators Your Classroom Management Plan

If you want the support of your administrators, they should be fully aware of exactly how you plan to deal with student behavior and under what circumstances you will send a student to their office. Before the school year begins, sit down with administrators and explain your goals for your classroom management efforts and what your rules, positive reinforcements, and corrective consequences will be.

Deal With Behavior Problems on Your Own Before Asking for Help

Whenever appropriate, you should attempt to handle a student's disruptive behavior on your own before you speak to parents or administrators about the situation. Both parents and administrators generally want to know that you have tried, on your own, to deal with the problem before you came to them.

Keep Documentation of Issues With Students

Keep documentation of how you deal with student behavior. When you contact parents or administrators, it is useful to have a complete record of what the issues are and the steps you have taken to deal with the student's behavior. Documentation can be kept on a simple card or incident sheet (see the sample on page 121).

Classroom Management Plan Letter to Parents

Dear Parent,

I am looking forward to working with your child this year. I also plan to work with you to ensure your child has the most successful school year possible.

An important part of your child being successful in my classroom is his/her learning how to behave appropriately. To help your child and the entire class, I have developed a classroom management plan:

Classroom Rules

- Follow directions.
- Keep hands, feet, and objects to yourself (no hitting, kicking, and so on).
- No swearing or teasing.

To encourage your child to follow these classroom rules, I will praise him/her, as well as send you good news notes and call you to share your child's successes. It is important that your child knows you support him/her behaving in my classroom, so I would appreciate you adding your own support when you get positive feedback from me.

However, if your child chooses to break a rule, the following steps will be taken:

- First time: Reminder
- Second time: Miss half of free choice
- Third time: Miss all of free choice
- Fourth time: Call parent
- Fifth time: Send to principal

Your support is very important. If I call you, I would appreciate you backing me up to ensure your child makes better choices in my classroom.

Please read this classroom management plan with your child, and then sign and return the form below. Here's to a great school year!

_____

I have read the classroom management plan and discussed it with my child.

Parent/Guardian Signature _____ Date _____

Comments:

Sample Student Issue Documentation

Student Name: Marcus Furlito

Date: 9/4/09   **Time:** 10:15   **Location:** Classroom

Issue: Marcus was talking out while I was teaching. When I corrected his behavior, he talked back.

Action Taken: I gave him the appropriate consequences from the management plan. Took him aside and spoke with him during the break.

The Importance of Parental Support

Before we go any further, let's examine why it is so important to get the support you need and deserve from parents. To start with, parents are obviously the most important people in a child's life. The parents' love, support, and approval are a fundamental need of each and every child. Since parents are number one in importance, they are also number one in their ability to influence and motivate their children to be successful in school.

To give you perspective on this point, consider this: if you were successful in school, ask yourself the following questions:

- Why did you behave at school?
- Why did you strive to succeed academically?

I would propose that if you are like most individuals who were successful in school, you answered that your parents played a major role in motivating your school efforts. Your students' parents possess the same potential!

The importance of parental support has been studied and validated for years by educational researchers.

> When parents are involved and support the teachers, simply put:
> - Students are better behaved (Henderson & Mapp, 2002).
> - Students' academic performance improves (Epstein, Clark, Salinas, & Sanders, 1997).

Given the importance of the parents' role in their children's success, it is a critical problem that so many teachers report having trouble building positive support relationships with many parents (Metropolitan Life Insurance Co., 2005). For many years, teachers have stated that the lack of parental support is a critical problem they face (Gibbs, 2005; Langdon, 1996).

Building Positive Relationships With Parents

Just as with some difficult students, you simply cannot assume that all of the students' parents will trust and support you. Again, many of them may have had very negative school experiences themselves. In addition, for most parents of difficult students, the overwhelming majority of the contact they have had with educators has been regarding what a "problem" their child is.

You have work to do to build positive, supportive relationships with these parents. Here are some steps you find effective teachers taking to build supportive relationships.

Contact Parents Before School Begins

As was discussed before, effective teachers proactively reach out to parents of difficult students by calling them before school begins. These teachers often reach out to all the parents by sending them a simple note introducing themselves and letting them know they are looking forward to working with their child (Jones, 2000).

Send Positive News to Parents

To repeat, the reality is that the overwhelming percentage of school–home communication is negative (Canter & Canter, 2001b). In general, teachers only contact parents when their child is having a problem. Once again, all this does is basically create a negative tone to the teacher–parent relationship.

> I cannot emphasize the next point strongly enough. In all my years of studying effective teachers, the key strategy they use to build support from parents is to consistently share positive news.

Sending positive news typically takes the form of short phone calls:

Hi, Ms. Hernandez. This is Ms. Saffa. I just wanted to let you know what a great day Jose had today. He worked extremely hard on all of his assignments and continues to be very cooperative. I enjoy having him in my class.

> A simple rule of thumb: make at least two positive contacts with parents each day, be it via phone call, email, or note. This will take a bit of time but can yield enormous benefits.

Make Home Visits

Another step effective teachers take that differentiates them from their peers is they make visits to their students' homes. Taking the time to go to a student's home and meet with parents or guardians demonstrates to everyone that you are not like the "other" teachers. By visiting the home you can go a long way to win over skeptical parents and get the support you need from them to help their child be successful (Mendler & Curwin, 1999).

You must determine what your district or school policy is on making home visits before you use this strategy. Of course, make sure such visits would in no way be unsafe for you to undertake alone.

> When dealing with a noncompliant student, one of the most effective tools to gain the support of his or her parents and build a positive relationship is to make a visit to the student's home as soon as possible during the school year.

Reach Out to Their Child

The relationship-building steps discussed in chapter 14, "Build Positive Relationships With Students," can also go a long way to building positive relationships with parents.

If parents hear that you called to see how their child was doing when he or she was sick, that you attended their child's recital, or their child talks about how caring you are, it can demonstrate to the parent that you are on their child's side.

Plan an Agenda When You Conference With Parents Regarding a Problem With Their Child

Don't underestimate how stressful it can be to speak with parents, especially when discussing issues such as their child's misbehavior. Knowing what to say and how to say it will go a long way in determining how productive the conversation will be.

You will want to maximize the possibility for a successful conversation with the parents by planning what you want to say and having notes at the ready whenever you speak, be it on the phone or face to face (Sprick, Garrison, & Howard, 1998).

Here are the points you will want to cover.

Begin With a Statement of Concern

Because discussing their child's issues can be stressful and upsetting to parents, it is important that you begin the conversation by showing your concern for the student rather than just bluntly stating the problem:

I want to talk with you because I'm concerned about Liza's behavior and how it is going to hinder her success at school.

Describe the Student's Behavior in Objective Terms

Be sure to avoid making vague, subjective, or judgmental comments to parents regarding their child's behavior:

He has a bad temper and does not get along with the other students.

Her attitude is not good and she is constantly in trouble.

She is always talking and disrupting everyone.

Such comments will set a negative tone and can make parents quite defensive.

It is much more useful to explain in specific, observable, nonjudgmental terms what their child did or did not do. If you are meeting face to face, show the parent your documentation to support your point.

I want to explain exactly what is happening. You can see from my records that during the last five days I have had to speak to Liza on six occasions. She keeps stating she does not want to do the work and does not have to.

Describe the Steps You Have Taken to Help Their Child

Parents will want to know what you, the teacher, have tried to do to help their child before you contacted them. Let them know all the steps you have attempted to solve the problem.

I have met with Liza and tried to get input from her as to how I can help her. I've gone over the assignments with her, and it is clear that when I'm working with her, she can do the work and it's not too hard.

As well, I've had Liza talk with the counselor and the vice principal. We all feel that it is in her best interests that you are involved with us in helping her get her assignments completed.

Get Parental Input on the Problem

Parents usually know their child better than anyone else does. They may have a good idea that could help solve the problem. Ask the parent questions such as:

Is this a problem your child has had before? If so, has anything helped your child cope with the problem?

Why do you feel your child is having this problem at school?

Is there anything going on at home that could be affecting your child's behavior that you think I should know about?

Discuss the Next Steps You Want to Take to Help Their Child

Let the parents know how you plan to move forward in helping their child be more successful:

I'm setting up a system where Liza can simply signal me if she is getting frustrated with an assignment, instead of getting upset or defiant. I'll then meet with her and help her get back on track. In addition, I'm going to let her earn bonus points toward extra free time for every assignment she completes on her own.

Discuss Why the Parents' Help Is Needed to Solve Their Child's Problem

Some parents may not comprehend how important their support is to helping their child's success at school. Discuss with the parents the significant impact their efforts can have in resolving their child's issues:

I will do all that I can to help Liza, but you're the most important person in her life, and your support with this issue is critical. She must know you will not tolerate her doing anything but her best effort in school.

I think it would be useful for Liza if we set up a plan that has her complete any work at home that she does not finish at school. How do you feel about that?

Express Your Confidence That the Problems Can Be Resolved

When you talk with parents regarding their child's problems, they will most likely be worried or concerned. It is important that you let the parents know you are confident there is a solution to the problem:

I have no doubt that if we work together, we can help Liza make better choices regarding completing her work. I'll bet she will dramatically improve when she knows we are on the same page and working as a team to help her.

Let the Parents Know That You Will Follow Up

Parents need to know that you are going to stay involved and in touch regarding their child's issue. Provide them a specific date for a follow-up call or note:

> *Ms. Cromartie, I'm going to call you next Thursday night and let you know how things are working out with Liza.*

Home–School Behavior Contract

With some difficult students you may find that a home–school behavior contract can be a highly effective strategy. In a home–school contract, the parents agree to back up your efforts by following through at home with positive rewards and disciplinary consequences depending on how their child behaves in your class.

A home–school contract is a collaborative effort between you and the parents. It is important that you have a clear plan of action in mind before you meet with a parent. Be prepared to discuss the following points with parents.

The Specific Behaviors You Expect From the Student

Tell the parent the exact behaviors you want to work on. Again, avoid value judgments that can make the parent defensive.

The Disciplinary Consequences the Parent Will Provide if the Student Does Not Behave

Discuss with the parents what actions they can take at home if their child does not behave that day in class. Typical consequences may include:

- Loss of electronic devices, such as cell phone, computer, video games, television
- Grounding in their room
- Loss of privileges

The Positive Consequences the Parents Will Provide if the Student Does Behave

Discuss with the parents what positive consequences they can give their child at home if he or she chooses to behave. Typical consequences include:

- Extra time on the computer, watching television, and so on
- Special snack
- Extra time with the parent
- The earned right to purchase something he or she wants

How You Will Communicate With the Parents

Tell the parents that you will send a note home each day to let them know how their child behaved that day. A positive report means the student will receive the predetermined reward, and a negative report means that the parent will provide the prearranged consequence.

Pulling It All Together

Never, repeat never, underestimate how important parental support can be for your success. Again, parents are simply the most important influential individuals in a child's life. Learn from effective teachers—take the steps needed to get all parents, especially those of difficult students, on your side and the results will be dramatic.

The Importance of Getting Support From Your Administrators

You can again have a profound impact on student behavior by utilizing the strategies we have discussed in the previous chapters. The reality is, though, that the support you do or do not receive from your administrators can dramatically impact how difficult it is going to be to deal with the behavioral issues of some of your noncompliant students.

Assistance With Defiant Students

As was previously mentioned, you may encounter noncompliant students who will openly defy your authority. You will want to remove those students from your classroom but may find they simply refuse to leave. Without administrative support, there is no way you can remove the students from your room.

You will need to proactively determine from your administrator what the school's procedure is to deal with severely disruptive students. Are you to call the office, the school's security squad, or someone else? Knowing that you have the backup you require is vital to ensure you have the confidence to stand your ground when students challenge your authority.

More Significant Disciplinary Consequences

As teachers, there are many disciplinary consequences available for you to utilize on your own, such as time out, time out in another classroom, missing recess, and calling parents.

> The reality is that with some students your disciplinary consequences may not carry the clout necessary to get their attention, and thus you're going to need the support of your administrators.

This is a thorny issue to address, because I work with all too many teachers who are in schools where there is a spoken or unspoken rule from the administrators that teachers should not send discipline problems to the office.

Let's address this issue.

First off, many administrators are reluctant to have teachers send students to the office because the teachers use him or her as a "dumping ground" for any student they don't feel like dealing with at that moment. That is obviously not an acceptable practice.

As a teacher, you should, under no circumstances, send a student to an administrator unless you have consistently followed the steps of the Behavior Management Cycle and complied with the guidelines of your classroom management plan. Only when those steps fail is it appropriate and in the best interests of the student and his or her classmates to be dealt with by an administrator.

Next, it is important that your school has a specific plan for what actions your administrator will take when a student is sent to the office. In many schools there is no plan for the disciplinary actions that will be taken by administrators and the result will be inconsistently provided consequences for disruptive behavior; one day a student will be simply counseled for ten minutes and sent back to class, whereas the next day another student will be sent home. Developing a schoolwide Assertive Discipline program will be addressed in more detail in the appendix.

Additional Positive Support

Most teachers view the administrator's role in dealing with students as that of the "bad guy." This is a shortsighted view. For many students, an administrator's positive attention can be a significant motivator to improve their behavior. For example:

- Arrange with your administrator for students who have improved their behavior to see him or her for a positive visit.

- Ask your administrator to make positive calls to parents of difficult students.

- Have your administrator make a special visit to the class to recognize students who have shaped up their behavior.

Counsel With the Parent or Student

You may have found it challenging trying to get some parents to meet with you regarding their child's behavior. A phone call from an administrator can provide the added encouragement an otherwise reluctant parent needs. Likewise, having an administrator sit in on a conference can demonstrate to parents how concerned the school is about their child's success and can be the key to motivating a parent to take action in helping solve a particular problem.

The same can be said for having an administrator spend a few minutes speaking with a student about his or her behavior. The weight of the administrator's position can carry the clout necessary to let some students know they need to choose more appropriate behavior at school.

▶ Key Points to Remember ◀

Don't buy into the myth of the good teacher; you need and deserve the support of administrators and parents in your efforts with students.

Share your classroom management plan with both parents and administrators.

Always attempt to deal with student behavior on your own before asking parents or administrators for assistance.

To gain parents' support, make positive contacts with them before school begins.

Consistently send home positive news to parents.

When appropriate, make home visits to sit down with parents.

When conferencing with parents, plan out the agenda and what you will say.

Administrator support is critical in providing additional disciplinary consequences and positive support to motivate difficult students to choose to behave.

Mentors, Coaches, and School Leadership Teams: Structures to Support Classroom Teachers' Behavior Management Efforts

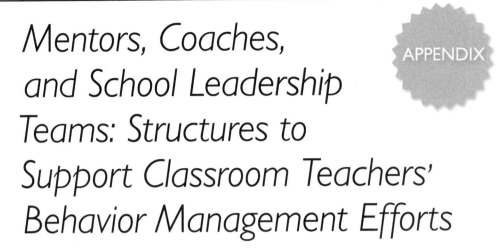

APPENDIX

Teachers' knowledge of best practices in classroom management is obviously a necessary first step in enabling them to create a safe, orderly classroom environment. The reality is though, that there are more steps needed to ensure teachers have the supports needed to maximize their ability to help students learn to behave appropriately in the classroom.

In this addendum we will provide an introduction to two important steps to increase teachers' success:

1. The Real Time Classroom Coaching Model—A new model of coaching to enable mentors, coaches, and others to assist teachers with raising their level of mastery in the use of classroom management skills

2. Establishing a schoolwide Assertive Discipline program—A model for school leadership teams to utilize to establish a schoolwide behavior management program that supports teachers' classroom efforts

An Introduction to the Real Time Classroom Coaching Model

Having teachers receive training in classroom management, be it reading books, watching videos, or attending live or online training, is an important first step to improve their classroom management skills. But experience and research teach us this step is often woefully insufficient.

> Just because teachers have been trained in research-based best practices does not mean they will utilize the practices effectively in their classrooms.

There are various reasons why, even after being trained, teachers do not effectively implement classroom management skills in their classrooms. Some teachers may not fully understand the concepts, others are resistant to change, and others are simply inconsistent in their application of the strategies they have learned (Scheeler, 2004).

There is, though, an additional issue I have found that profoundly impacts why so many teachers have difficulty implementing effective classroom management skills, no matter how much training they have received.

> You cannot expect teachers to learn classroom management skills and simply go back to their classrooms and competently implement these strategies without regular *effective feedback* from mentors, coaches, administrators, or peers.

My firsthand experience with this reality resulted in my development of the Real Time Classroom Coaching Model.

The Birth of the Real Time Classroom Coaching Model

The development of the Real Time Classroom Coaching Model began as a result of my experiences teaching a course on classroom management for beginning teachers at a local university in the late 1990s. In this course, I had the opportunity to work closely with a small group of teachers, both instructing them in a weekly seminar and directly supervising them in their classrooms.

At the start of the course, I taught the students the basic Assertive Discipline model presented in this book. The teachers quickly grasped the basic concepts of the model and expressed their belief that it would serve to be a major improvement over the other classroom management approaches they were unsuccessfully attempting to implement in their classrooms.

In order to ensure the teachers understood the new model, I thoroughly tested them on their knowledge of the concepts and how to apply them with their students. All of the teachers passed the examination with flying colors. It was obvious they had a thorough understanding of the conceptual ideas they were being taught. I was interested in visiting the teachers' classrooms to observe how effective they were with their students using the new management model.

To my chagrin, what I observed as I went from classroom to classroom was disheartening. Though the teachers understood in theory the steps to effectively manage their students' behavior, their application of these steps was a totally different story. It became crystal clear to me that simply teaching beginning teachers new classroom management concepts in a seminar in no way translated to their effectively using them in their classrooms.

It was obvious that I needed to provide mentoring to these teachers on their use of the classroom management skills. I began my mentoring efforts using the standard approach most educators utilize, which is to sit in the back of the class, script out what takes place, and then at a later time sit down with the teacher and go over what was observed.

What I found was when I met with the teachers, they recognized what they should have done differently with their students and verbally indicated how they would change their responses in the classroom. When I again returned to observe them, to my dismay I found that, fundamentally, nothing had changed. The traditional model of mentoring rarely resulted in the teachers improving their use of the classroom management skills they had been taught.

An Eye-Opening Experience

Finally, the despair of one of my teachers resulted in me "throwing out the book" on traditional mentoring methods and improvising another approach—*real-time coaching*.

It began one morning when I entered a teacher's classroom only to find her close to tears due to her inability to get her students to listen to her. I had to think on my feet and do something to quickly help this teacher so she would not have a complete meltdown in front of her students.

When the students left for recess, the teacher broke down and asked for any suggestions. It was at this point obvious that this teacher was unable to control the classroom on her own. Since it was not appropriate for me to take over her classroom, I had to find some way to get her through the next part of the day.

Suddenly, the proverbial light bulb came on: maybe the next best thing for me to do was to sit in the back of the classroom and coach her on how to handle the students' behavior. On the spur of the moment, I told the teacher the following:

Here's how I'm going to help you. I'm going to be in the back of the room and will coach you on how to use the classroom management skills you were taught in our seminar on the Behavior Management Cycle. I want you to keep an eye on me as much as possible.

When you see me raise one finger, I want you to stop what you are doing and tell the students the exact directions you want them to follow at that moment.

When you see me raise two fingers, I want you to immediately look for students who are following your directions and narrate their behavior.

When you see me raise three fingers, I want you to immediately give disruptive students consequences from your discipline plan.

When the students returned, what took place was a true eye-opener. I found myself constantly cueing the teacher by most frequently raising two or three fingers to indicate that she needed to provide positive feedback to students or to firmly respond to students' off-task, disruptive behavior.

At first she was tentative about following my feedback, but she soon caught on to what I was after. The turning point came when one of her most difficult students became highly disruptive. As the student kept talking out, I kept raising three fingers, indicating that she should provide him with the disciplinary consequences he was choosing by his disruptive behavior.

Within a few minutes the student had reached the point where the next consequence for disrupting would be to go to the principal's office. When he again yelled out and I again raised three fingers signaling her to act, she at first hesitated and gave me a look that said, "Do you *really* think I should send him out?" When I nodded yes, she walked up to the student, looked him in the eye, and firmly told him he had chosen to go to the principal's office and he should go right away!

The student was obviously shocked by how his teacher had suddenly stood her ground, as were his classmates. As the student, to everyone's surprise, quietly left the room, you could feel the change come over the classroom—the students recognized that their teacher finally meant business and would no longer tolerate them not listening to her.

I was stunned by the transformation I observed in the teacher's behavior in the short time I was giving her real-time feedback. It was obvious that providing her immediate feedback had proven to be a dramatic tool to quickly increase her effectiveness in managing the classroom.

When I met with the teacher shortly after the real-time feedback session had ended, she quickly validated my perceptions. Obviously excited by the change in her students' behavior, she shared with me the significant impact receiving immediate feedback had had on her.

First, with relief in her voice, she exclaimed, "I actually got the students to listen to me—I never thought I could do that!"

When I explored what she had done differently with the students to produce the change, she responded, "Through your feedback I was more positive with the students than

I have ever been. I made more positive comments to the students in twenty minutes than I usually do in an entire morning or day, and for the first time I didn't just threaten and argue with the students—I simply provided them consequences every time they chose to be disruptive."

As we continued to reflect on what had transpired in her classroom, she went on to add, "I thought I understood what you taught in class about the need to be positive and firm, but I was wrong. Through following the immediate feedback you were giving me, I could experience firsthand how consistently I have to respond in order to effectively motivate the students to listen to me."

The positive impact the real-time feedback session had on this teacher was driven home to me by an email she sent me the next day:

> Yesterday's session enabled me to turn my classroom around. Today I was finally able to spend my time teaching and not disciplining my students. I'm back in touch with why I entered this profession! Consider using the immediate feedback method with the other teachers in our seminar—I'll bet it will be an invaluable experience for them too!

Refining the Model: Using the "Bug in the Ear"

Based on the dramatic impact real-time feedback had in the aforementioned teacher's classroom, I began using the approach whenever I mentored other new teachers in my seminar. With most of the teachers, the results were equally impressive. In only one observation and feedback session lasting approximately one hour, the vast majority of the struggling teachers were able to demonstrate significant improvement in their ability to handle their students' behavior.

Most impressive to me was the fact that when I went back for future visits to the teachers' classrooms, they were all still demonstrating a higher level of competence in their use of classroom management skills than when I first worked with them. In the follow-up real-time feedback sessions, most of the teachers were able to utilize the feedback and continued to improve their effectiveness in dealing with classroom management issues.

As I continued to work with teachers using the real-time feedback model, it became apparent to me that there could be, at times, some shortcomings to simply using hand signals to cue the teacher. Sometimes the teacher would not look at me at appropriate times, and there were instances when I wanted to direct the teacher's attention to particular students but was unable to do so.

In reviewing the literature on teacher training, I found several references to mentors/coaches using a "bug in the ear" one-way audio transmitter to provide feedback to the teachers with whom they were working. The use of this low-tech, low-cost (approximately $40 per set) walkie-talkie enabled me to sit in the back of the room and, as appropriate, give specific feedback.

In addition, the use of a bug in the ear gave me the ability to provide the teachers with positive feedback, for example, "Excellent job correcting students!" Obviously, the ability to provide such positive feedback was of equal importance to my efforts to help improve the teachers' mastery of classroom management skills.

An important point I quickly learned was that if I kept my comments to a few key words, such as "Give clear directions," "Narrate students," or "Correct off-task students," teachers were not distracted by them and quickly got comfortable with the use of the bug in the ear.

Just recently, the coaches I've been working with have begun to provide real-time feedback using their cell phones with Bluetooth® connections. The coach simply has the teacher put a Bluetooth connection in his ear, and then at the beginning of the feedback session, the coach calls him to establish the audio connection. The coach then simply talks to the teacher as anyone would via cell phone.

Real-Time Feedback

What my initial experiences with real-time coaching made me aware of was the importance of providing teachers with effective and immediate feedback, and that this is an overlooked tool that is vital to helping teachers improve their implementation of effective classroom skills (Scheeler, 2006). As with learning any new skill, mastery of effective classroom practices is dramatically impacted by the quality and quantity of the feedback the teachers receive.

If you are like most educators, you have some basic knowledge of the guidelines to follow to provide teachers with effective feedback.

Feedback Is Given on Best Practices That Teachers Already Have Been Trained In

The feedback must be provided on the best practice that the teacher thoroughly understands. It would obviously not be productive to attempt to give a teacher feedback on her ability to manage students' behavior unless she had comprehensive training in effective classroom management skills.

Feedback Is Provided by a Coach Who Has Expertise in the Effective Implementation of the Best Practice

Coaches obviously must have expertise in the best practice on which they will give teachers feedback on their performance (Sprick et al., 2006). You will not be able to help a teacher master an effective classroom management strategy if you don't know how to implement it yourself.

Feedback Is Provided on Specific Performance Criteria

You and the teacher need to establish specific performance criteria upon which to base the feedback on the teacher's use of classroom management skills.

Feedback Is Both Positive and Constructive

You need to provide teachers with feedback on both what they are doing that is effective and what they need to do to improve in areas where they are ineffective (Scheeler, 2004; Van Houten, 1980). For example, when you observe them dealing effectively with student behavior, you will want to point this out as well as discuss what they can do more effectively when they have difficulties.

Feedback Is Immediate

In addition to these guidelines, there is one critical aspect of effective feedback that has been long overlooked by coaches working with teachers. What we know about learning theory is that when anyone is attempting to learn a new skill, the more immediate the feedback, the higher the learning curve. It is no different with teachers.

In reality, the feedback teachers most often receive from a coach is delayed. For example, a teacher is observed in her classroom, and the coach will then meet with her half an hour, an hour, or even a day later to discuss what was observed and provide her feedback on her efforts.

> Research clearly indicates that giving teachers delayed feedback is not nearly as effective as providing it to them immediately or in real time (Scheeler, 2006).

Far and away, the feedback that has the most potential impact is given to teachers in a nondistracting manner while they are in the classroom actually teaching.

The Tennis Coach Analogy

The importance of real-time feedback in improving teachers' classroom skills can best be illustrated by the analogy of how an effective tennis coach goes about improving the skills of a player.

In the past you may have taken a tennis lesson (or other athletic lesson) from a coach in order to learn or improve your skills. Throughout the lesson, as you hit the ball, the coach would provide real-time feedback on your efforts, giving encouragement and suggestions such as "Put your racquet back," "Keep your eye on the ball," and "Good follow through." The immediate feedback was critical to you in improving your skills.

Now, on the other hand, could you imagine if the coach observed you hitting the ball for an entire lesson without saying a word? Then, be it an hour or a day later, the coach sat down with you and discussed what took place during the lesson—pointing out that you forgot to get your racquet back sooner and you did not keep your eye on the ball. You can easily imagine how much less effective this delayed feedback would be from that provided in real time.

In reality, the feedback most coaches provide to teachers is analogous to that provided by the tennis coach in the second scenario. The delayed feedback, again, has serious limitations; immediate real-time feedback is dramatically more useful in improving teacher mastery.

The following feature box shows a sample of a real-time feedback session in which the coach is giving feedback on the use of the Behavior Management Cycle using the bug-in-the-ear method.

Sample Real-Time Feedback Session

Teacher: Okay class, let's get started. And I want to be clear—I don't want any more issues when I'm talking like we've been having.

(Some students are listening, but many are talking and off task.)

Coach: Give explicit directions.

Teacher: What I mean is that when I'm talking, I expect to see all of you paying attention with nothing in your hands but a pencil and no talking.

Coach: Good directions.

(The teacher does not provide any positive feedback to students who get on task.)

Coach: Narrate behavior.

Teacher: James, Jose, and Vanessa have their eyes on me and are not talking. That is what I expect.

(Teacher begins the lesson and gets so involved with the content that she does not monitor the students' behavior and soon a number of students start talking.)

Coach: Narrate behavior.

Teacher: I see Juanita is paying attention without talking, and so are Denzel and Cary.

(After the teacher's response, all but one of the students get on task. The student continues talking and disrupting his classmates, but the teacher does not respond to his behavior.)

Coach: Correct the student who is talking.

Teacher: James, the direction was to pay attention without talking. That is your warning.

(Teacher resumes lesson, and all the students are engaged for a while, but as the teacher continues to simply lecture to the class, students begin to get bored, off task, and disruptive.)

(Teacher spontaneously monitors the students' behavior and provides positive feedback to on-task students.)

Teacher: Table three students all have their eyes on me and are not talking— the same for tables four and five.

Coach: Excellent narration.

Advantages of the Real Time Classroom Coaching Model

Using the Real Time Classroom Coaching Model (with teachers who have been trained in basic Assertive Discipline skills) is an important new tool that educators can utilize in their efforts to improve the classroom management skills of today's teachers.

Advantages for Coaches

There are several significant advantages to using the Real Time Classroom Coaching Model for any coach, mentor, or administrator (herein referred to as "coach") who is working with teachers to help them improve their classroom performance.

Coaches Are Empowered to Assist the Teacher During the Classroom Observation

Most coaches find one of the more disheartening aspects of their role is to have to sit by helplessly and watch a teacher's lesson or class fall apart when there is nothing they can do. Through the use of real-time feedback, the coach will be empowered to, when appropriate, meaningfully intervene during the observation. Using immediate feedback has the potential to help guide a struggling teacher to take the necessary steps to salvage his or her lesson.

Coaches Can Take Advantage of Teachable Moments During the Classroom Observation

There have likely been many times when you were observing a teacher, and a student said something or an instructional issue came up and you said to yourself, "I wish I could point out what to say or do at this moment." In other words, you had to deal with the frustration of not being able to take advantage of a valuable teachable moment that could have helped the teacher's development.

Having the ability to communicate immediately with the teacher allows you to take advantage of the teachable moments that may arise. You will never again have to sit back in frustration while missing an opportunity to help a teacher learn a valuable classroom lesson.

Teachers Are More Likely to Implement the Coach's Suggestions

As a coach, you have most likely found that often teachers simply do not implement your suggestions or do so in an inadequate manner. There may be many reasons for this, but usually it is a direct result of the structure of the traditional coaching model. Here is what I mean.

You are surely aware that in the traditional coaching model, the teacher does not have the opportunity to learn about or practice the changes you feel he or she should make until long after you first observe an ineffective practice.

- First, there is the delay from the time that you observe the teacher's ineffective practice until you can meet with the teacher and make the appropriate suggestions for how to improve the classroom practice.

- Second, there is another delay from the time you make the suggestions until the teacher can implement them with his or her students. These delays allow the teacher's memory to fade and too often your suggestions are poorly implemented, if at all.

In the Real Time Classroom Coaching Model, your suggestions can be implemented immediately. If the teacher starts losing control of the class and you tell her to correct the disruptive students, the teacher implements your suggestion, sees the positive effect on the students, is reinforced for the improvement, and will be much more likely to continue to implement the improved practice in the future.

Advantages for Teachers

There are several other important advantages to using the Real Time Classroom Coaching Model for teachers who have received training in Assertive Discipline skills.

The Ability to More Rapidly Learn How to Effectively Utilize Best Practices

There is one profound advantage for teachers whose coaches effectively utilize real-time feedback: they are able to learn how to use best practices they have had training in with their students in a dramatically expedited manner. There are several reasons this is so.

Immediate Feedback From the Coach. First, as was mentioned earlier, much as having a skilled coach giving you effective immediate feedback can dramatically improve your tennis or golf game, the same can be said for the impact a coach giving such real-time feedback can have on the development of a teacher's classroom skills. Again, as the research clearly states, there is no substitute for immediate, specific, positive, and constructive feedback, such as is provided in this model, to improve the learning curve for teachers (Scheeler, 2004).

Opportunity to Experience the Impact of Effective Practice. In addition, there is an old saying: *there is no teacher like experience.* Through receiving immediate feedback from a trained coach, a teacher can be guided to experience for the first time what it feels like to use classroom strategies effectively.

A teacher who is unable to motivate students to get and stay on task during a lesson can be guided to utilize effective behavior management skills, and for the first time "feel what it takes" to be in charge of the classroom. Seeing, hearing, and feeling what effective practice is like can leave a lasting impression and have a dramatic impact on the teacher's professional growth.

Advantages for Students

The ultimate beneficiaries of the Real Time Classroom Coaching Model are the students. We all know the skill level of the teacher is a critical factor determining the academic success of the students. Don't the students deserve to have you, the coach, do all you can to help their teacher reach his or her full professional potential?

When all is said and done, the final rationale for the use of the Real Time Classroom Coaching Model can be found by looking at another analogy.

The Medical Doctor Analogy

Can you imagine a supervising medical doctor sitting passively by while the intern or resident she is working with conducts a medical procedure in a manner that is harmful to the patient's health? Of course not!

Well then, why is it okay for a coach to sit by passively while the teacher she is working with is dealing with her class in a manner that is harmful to the students' emotional or intellectual health and simply allow it to continue?

Supporting Struggling Teachers

Several years ago I began training mentors, coaches, and school administrators in how to use the Real Time Classroom Coaching Model. The response from both coaches and the teachers with whom they worked was dramatic.

Most coaches reported that using real-time coaching significantly increased their ability to assist teachers with classroom management issues. They reported that with only one or two sessions of real-time feedback, most teachers were able to meaningfully improve their ability to deal with student behavior.

Teachers' feedback was equally positive. The overwhelming number of teachers reported that the real-time feedback sessions were powerful learning experiences that were extremely useful in improving their classroom practice.

It is my sincere belief that the expanded use of the Real Time Classroom Coaching Model has the potential to be a significant tool to help improve the professional ability of countless teachers.

▶ Key Points to Remember ◀

Teachers need effective feedback to improve their mastery of skills.

Feedback needs to be provided in real time—in other words, immediately.

Feedback needs to be provided by trained coaches.

Providing feedback in real time has advantages for the coach, teacher, and students.

An Introduction to Establishing a Schoolwide Assertive Discipline Program

All too often teachers who are struggling with behavior issues are working in schools that have poorly designed or ineffectively implemented schoolwide behavior management programs that make the teachers' challenges even more daunting.

Why So Many Schools' Behavior Management Efforts Are Ineffective

Let's examine why so many schools struggle with issues related to student behavior.

Staff Believe They Have to Tolerate Disruptive Behavior

In schools where students' behavior is a problem, you will often find the staff believing their students have such severe problems that they can't get them to behave appropriately (Canter & Canter, 2001a).

He has such emotional and behavioral problems, we can't expect him to act like the other students.

Her parents are so dysfunctional; no wonder she is such a behavior problem.

How can we expect the students to behave coming from such a violent, poverty-ridden neighborhood?

As a result of these beliefs, the staff feels they have to tolerate disruptive behavior and typically, out of frustration, let the "little things" slide. These little things typically include such disruptive behaviors as talking inappropriately in class, running in the halls, students teasing one another, littering, and graffiti.

Unfortunately, experience teaches us that letting the little things slide typically will lead to "big things" happening. Here is what I mean.

Letting little things slide leads to bigger problems is a key concept of a popular theory of crime prevention called the *broken-window theory*. The theory suggests that when a building is abandoned and has all of its windows unbroken, there is usually little vandalism to the premises. If, though, just one window is broken and left unattended, soon many or all of the windows will be broken by vandals (Gladwell, 2002).

Let me elaborate. Simply seeing one broken window gives vandals the idea that it is okay to break other windows and further damage the building. Soon, if such antisocial behavior is allowed to continue, it will breed even greater problems and eventually the neighborhood can cross the tipping point into social decay.

What does the broken-window theory have to do with a school's behavior management issues? If educators believe they are helpless to deal with the students' behavior and thus have to let the little things slide (for example, talking or running in the halls), then students perceive they are given de facto permission to cause even bigger problems, such as defiance, fighting, or bullying. All too often, if disruptive behavior is not addressed firmly and fairly, schools can go beyond the "tipping point" and become an environment that is not supportive to student learning or to the staff's well-being.

When all is said and done, if educators believe their students have such problems that they cannot motivate them to choose to behave at school, in all likelihood serious behavior problems will unfortunately be the order of the day.

An Ineffective Schoolwide Behavior Management Plan

Your school probably has some form of a schoolwide behavior management plan that is supposed to set guidelines for how to establish a safe, orderly school environment. If your school is struggling with student behavior, why isn't the plan working?

The Plan Simply Isn't Used

In too many schools, the schoolwide behavior plan is basically a useless piece of paper that most staff members are not familiar with or, if they are, they simply do not follow its guidelines.

It's a Top-Down Mandate

In many cases, the administration has tried to mandate a schoolwide behavior management plan without the involvement and support of the rest of the staff. Without staff buy in, most plans are never accepted and utilized (Colvin, 2007).

Schools Try a Quick-Fix Approach

Often a school staff gets fed up with the disruptive behavior of students and quickly creates a behavior management plan to handle the problem. There are no structures put in place to ensure the plan is implemented effectively, consistently, or evaluated for effectiveness.

There is no quick fix to schoolwide behavior management. Effective plans take at least a year to develop, implement, and evaluate (Sprague, Sugai, & Walker, 1998).

An effectively developed and implemented schoolwide behavior management plan is the foundation of any school's effort to establish a safe, orderly, and positive school environment. Without such a blueprint for action, a school staff's efforts are basically doomed to failure.

Emphasis Is on a "Get Tough" Policy

Many staffs believe the answer to their school's behavior issues is to crack down on the disruptive students. They believe if they "get tougher" with the consequences they provide, they will shape up the students.

The reality is that disciplinary consequences may temporarily stop disruptive behavior, but if this is all that is attempted with students, they will eventually backfire and result in even further problems (Sprague & Walker, 2005). You simply cannot "hard nose" today's students and expect they will choose to behave.

Disciplinary Consequences Are Ineffective

Many staffs use disciplinary consequences that simply do not motivate the students to improve their behavior (Walker & Eaton-Walker, 2000). Either the consequences are not appropriately implemented, such as students are assigned detention but there is no follow up if the students do not attend, or consequences are simply ineffective, such as with an overreliance on out-of-school suspension.

Staff Is Not Trained in Behavior Management Best Practices

As has been presented in earlier chapters, many teachers have not had effective training in the behavior management skills that are critical to their success. In all probability, the reality is equally grim for your school's administrators who receive minimal training on how they need to deal with student behavior from their perspective.

When you examine the consequences of educators not being properly trained in effective behavior management skills, you often find a school where the following occurs:

- Expectations for student behavior are unclear.
- Response to student behavior is overwhelmingly negative.
- Response to students' inappropriate behavior is inconsistent.
- Staff members are not able to build positive relationships with students.
- Staff members are not able to build positive relationships with parents.

Staff Efforts Are Not Driven by Data

When behavior is a problem at a school, there is typically a lack of data on the problem behavior. Most schools that struggle with student behavior base their management efforts on their perceptions and feelings about what the problems are, and what is or is not working to fix the problems (Sprague & Walker, 2005).

Educators have become aware of the importance of data to drive instructional issues. The same can be said for the importance of data to drive behavior management issues. Basing schoolwide behavior efforts solely on staff perceptions simply does not produce effective results. All staff actions must be based on systematic gathering and analysis of data, such as what are the staff's issues regarding student behavior, which students are the problems, where do problems occur, and what interventions are working.

Schools Can Transform Their Learning Climate

Thousands of schools around the country have turned around their learning environment by using the concepts and skills presented in the Assertive Discipline program. Schools can transform their learning climate, dramatically reduce disruptive behavior, and increase academic achievement by implementing research-based best practices.

Schools that utilize effective schoolwide behavior practices do the following:

- **Increase student achievement**—Numerous studies at all grade and socioeconomic levels clearly indicate that students at schools with effective management programs have higher standardized test scores than their peers at more disruptive schools (Horner, Sugai, Eber, & Lewandowski, 2004; Horner, Sugai, Todd, & Lewis-Palmer, 2005).

- **Reduce classroom disruptions**—At schools that implement effective schoolwide programs, studies indicate that the disruptive behavior in classrooms is reduced by at least 50 percent (Scott & Barrett, 2004). In addition, there is a corresponding increase in students' time on task.

- **Reduce office referrals**—The number of students referred to the office for behavior issues drops dramatically at schools that implement effective schoolwide programs. Most schools report a minimum 50 percent reduction the first year with continued improvement over a three-year period (Luiselli, Putnam, Handler, & Feinberg, 2005).

- **Increase staff satisfaction**—Along with student behavior improving, so does the job satisfaction of staff at schools that implement effective schoolwide programs. Studies indicate all staff, including teachers, administrators, and support personnel, report they experience less stress and frustration than before the program began.

Attributes of Schools With Effective Schoolwide Behavior Management Efforts

Let's look at what differentiates schools that have effective schoolwide behavior management efforts from similar schools that are struggling.

High Expectations

When you talk with the staff of schools that have effective behavior management programs, what you find is a group of educators who have dramatically higher expectations in their ability to positively influence the behavior of all students, including those with problems, than you typically find in most schools. Basically, the beliefs and expectations of these educators can be summed up as follows:

We will not tolerate students engaging in any behavior that stops educators from teaching, is harmful to other students, or is not in the best interests of the students. When we all work together, we can motivate all of the students to meet our expectations for appropriate behavior at our school.

When you observe the staff in action, it becomes clear that it is a group of educators who under no circumstances are going to let the little things slide. Their expectations are backed up with clear, firm, and fair action whenever students choose for any reason not to comply with their expectations for appropriate behavior in class and out. In other words, students get a clear message that all the adults at school mean business when it comes to expecting them to make positive choices regarding how they behave at school.

To begin the process of transforming your school environment, you need to examine your beliefs about your ability to influence student behavior. To do so, I want to elaborate on the concepts discussed in chapter 3, "Hold High Expectations," that bear repeating when looking at schoolwide behavior issues.

Does your staff believe they are capable of motivating all the students, including those with problems, to choose to behave appropriately? Or does the staff simply believe it can't be done?

I propose if your school is struggling with behavior issues, the majority of your staff believes the latter, because you have so many students with problems, such as emotional, behavioral, familial, and socioeconomic, that you simply can't influence them to behave as you want.

In the service of improving your school's behavioral issues, I want to challenge your staff's negative expectations regarding their ability to positively influence your students' behavior. Follow along as I have you engage in an exercise that most educators report they find quite eye-opening.

I want to start this exercise with a question:

> Do the problems your students have really prevent your staff from being able to motivate them to control their behavior and to do what you need them to?

If you're like many educators struggling with behavior problems at your school, you will probably answer yes. The answer is logical given the issues at your school.

Just for a moment, consider this: if you have negative expectations of your ability to motivate your students to behave, you are, in reality, simply wrong. I propose you and your fellow educators can and have been able to motivate your students, even those troubled with the aforementioned problems, to choose to behave appropriately at your school. Let me elaborate on my thesis.

The Standardized-Testing Day Phenomenon

This is again a concept that was discussed in chapter 3, "Hold High Expectations," but needs repeating.

Think back to the last day you had your students take high-stakes, mandated achievement tests. Did the students, including those you and colleagues consider problems, behave the way you wanted them to on these days? The answer most likely is a resounding, "Of course they did!"

What phenomenon occurred that enabled educators, who are typically so frustrated by their inability to get their troubled students to stop disrupting, to get the same students to quickly follow their directions and get and stay on task?

The dramatic improvement in behavior is the result of one simple, yet profound change: *Bottom line, on testing days, the entire staff believes that what is occurring is so important that the students must cooperate and behave appropriately. The staff raises the bar for what behavior is acceptable and the students respond accordingly.*

The question is simply this: if your staff can get the students, even those with problems, to do what you want on testing days, why can't you get them to do what you want any other day?

Is what occurs in the classroom on testing days any more important to your students' future than what takes place each and every other day?

In order for you to fully understand the testing day phenomenon and how you can produce the same results day in and day out, let's examine what you and your colleagues do differently that produces the results you want and need.

You Believe It Is Okay to Raise the Bar. On testing days, you believe you are justified in raising the bar regarding the behavior you expect from students. You are not concerned about being too firm or strict, concerns that plague many schools' behavior management efforts. Your priority is to make sure all students, even those with problems, simply behave appropriately and take the test without disrupting.

You Clearly Communicate Your Expectations. Your staff's decision to raise the bar is reflected in how they relate and respond to the students. They begin by letting the students know, in no uncertain terms, exactly how they are expected to behave.

During the state test all students are expected to take the test, keep their eyes on their own paper, stay seated, and not talk. No one assumes students know how to behave. Instead, all the staff clearly teach the students exactly how they want them to do it.

You Provide More Positive Support. Contrary to popular belief that the only way educators can get students to do what they want is through heavy-handed intimidation, the opposite typically occurs. In most schools on testing days, the staff goes out of its way to recognize and respond to the appropriate behavior of students, be it with praise or special rewards.

You Will Not Let the Little Things Slide and Are Prepared to Set Firm Limits on Disruptive Behavior. On testing days you will not let the little things slide, like inappropriate talking or goofing around. There is no way the school is going to cross the tipping point described in the broken-window theory and devolve into a disruptive environment on those days.

Through words and actions, the staff lets all the students, including those with problems, know that they mean business and will set and enforce limits if any student chooses to be disruptive. Your students quickly sense the change in attitude and improve their behavior.

Raise the Bar at Your School

Since you have been able to stop letting the little things slide by raising the bar in the past, I have a question for you: why can't you do the same consistently in the future? Why can't you take the same steps you took on those days you were so much more effective, and apply them day in and day out so that you can create a school environment where students can learn and educators can teach free from the burden of dealing with disruptive behavior?

Administrators Who "Walk the Walk"

Let's be clear, schools where student behavior is not an issue have effective administrators—period. The research is clear: for a school's behavior management efforts to be effective, the administrators must be 100 percent committed to leading the charge (Kam, Greenberg, & Walls, 2003). If this does not occur, the odds are slim to none that any change will happen. When you look at the attributes of effective administrators, what do you see?

Effective Administrators Raise the Bar for Acceptable Behavior

Effective administrators let it be known to one and all that they are ready, willing, and able to work with the staff to raise the bar for acceptable behavior and thus turn around the learning environment at the school. They will "talk the talk" by telling staff, students, and parents that they simply will not let the little things slide and that they believe all students will be taught that appropriate behavior is expected at all times both in and out of the classroom (Jenson, Rhode, Evans, & Morgan, 2006).

Effective Administrators Establish and Support a Behavior Management Committee

Research indicates that effective schools establish what is known as a behavior management committee to guide the school's behavior management efforts. The committee is made up of key staff such as administrators, teachers, and support personnel (Colvin, 2007).

It is critical that the administrators take the lead in meeting with the staff, explain the need for the committee, and get key staff to join. Once the committee is established, the administrators must take all the steps needed to support its actions by participating regularly in the meetings, backing the plans the committee develops, and giving verbal and written support for its actions to the rest of the staff, parents, and students (see page 150 for more details).

Effective Administrators Model How to Build Relationships With Students

Effective administrators are clear role models for how staff are to deal with students. They are out and about in classrooms and the common areas, and can be counted on to provide overwhelming positive feedback to students who are behaving appropriately.

On the other hand, students know they had better watch out if these administrators observe them misbehaving or are sent to them because they caused a problem at school (Jenson et al., 2006).

Under no circumstances when they observe the little things sliding at school will they sit back and not respond. Students know these administrators are "cool" if you behave, and "mean business" if you don't.

Effective Administrators Demonstrate "Withitness" With Staff

Studies of teachers who are effective in managing their classroom indicate that they demonstrate to their students that they have "withitness." *Withitness* means that the teacher is at all times on top of how the students are behaving, has eyes in the back of her head, so to speak, and clearly lets students know this is so (Kounin, 1970).

Effective administrators demonstrate that they are with it when it comes to how the staff is dealing with student behavior and implementing the school's plan. There can be no doubt in anyone's mind that the administrators are on top of all aspects of the schoolwide behavior management program.

Effective Administrators Hold Staff Accountable for Supporting the Schoolwide Efforts

Effective administrators make it perfectly clear to each and every staff member their expectations that staff will be on board with the efforts to improve the behavior of students at the school.

Just as with students, if staff members give 100 percent to supporting the school plan, these administrators will provide them with overwhelming positive feedback and support. On the other hand, if they observe any staff member letting the little things slide or not doing their part to support the school's management plan, the response will be clear, firm, and unequivocal (Colvin, 2007).

A Behavior Management Committee That Guides the Schoolwide Efforts

The efforts of schools with effective behavior management are not driven by a top-down mandate from the administrators, but a collective effort led by a behavior management committee. This committee is the heart and soul of the school's management efforts (Sprague & Golly, 2005).

The behavior management committee is made up of representatives of all the key stakeholders at the school: administration, counselors, teachers, and support staff. The functions of an effective committee are wide ranging and will include the following:

- Developing the schoolwide behavior management plan
- Generating staff buy in for the plan

- Planning the schoolwide data collection system that tracks behavior problems, and evaluating the data on an ongoing basis
- Planning appropriate inservice training for school staff
- Providing assistance to staff members who are having difficulty with management issues
- Keeping track of students with chronic or severe behavior problems and helping develop individualized interventions for them
- Suggesting adjustments and changes to the schoolwide behavior management systems as needed

The behavior management committee meets on a regular basis, typically monthly. Through its efforts it serves as a firm rudder to steer the school's management efforts toward consistent success.

A Comprehensive, Research-Based Schoolwide Behavior Plan

Effective schoolwide efforts are guided by a comprehensive schoolwide behavior management plan. The plan needs to include specifics such as the following:

- Expectations for student behavior in all areas of the school
- Positive incentives to motivate students to behave
- Consequences students will receive when they are sent to the administrator
- Consequences for disrupting in the halls, cafeteria, and yard
- Interventions for chronic and severe behavior problems
- Tardy policy
- Weapons and drug policy

Staff Trained to Use Assertive Discipline Strategies Throughout the School

At effective schools, no staff members are ever forced to fend for themselves and sink or swim based on the behavior management skills they bring with them to their job. It is not assumed that everyone knows the best behavior management practices for their position.

Ongoing training in effective behavior management skills is the name of the game for all staff. We're not talking about the once and done, so-called "dog and pony show" where the expert comes in, tells staff members what to do, and then leaves. The behavior management training successful staff receive is comprehensive and geared to the needs of the educator (Taylor-Greene et al., 1997).

Staff not only get trained in basic behavior management skills but also advanced skills to enable them to deal with students with more difficult problems, as well as the critical skills needed to get the parents of these students on board.

Staff Has a Common Skill Set to Deal With Student Behavior

The upshot of such an effective model of training is that each and every member of the staff will speak the same language and be on the same page when it comes to how to deal with students' behavior. The training will enable the staff to do the following:

- Recognize that all students are capable of behaving appropriately and accept the responsibility to take all steps necessary to ensure they learn to do so
- Establish an effective classroom management plan that includes rules, disciplinary consequences, and positive incentives
- Teach students appropriate behavior in both the classroom and common areas of the school
- Clearly communicate to students at all times how they are expected to behave in order to be successful at school
- Monitor student behavior and provide consistent positive feedback (3:1 ratio positive to negative) to students who choose to comply with expectations
- Monitor student behavior and quickly provide corrective action in accordance with the school policy in a calm, respectful manner when students choose to misbehave
- Take the steps necessary to build trusting relationships with all students, especially those who are at risk
- Take the steps necessary to build trusting relationships with the students' parents or guardians, especially those who are at risk

Effective Schools Use a Continuum of Behavioral Intervention

The staff members at effective schools recognize that there simply is not one approach to behavior management that works for all students. Research indicates that effective schools utilize a continuum of interventions depending on the needs of the students.

All Efforts Are Data Driven

Meaningful change begins with a profound relationship with what's so. Just as any effective school uses data on student learning to guide its instructional efforts, the same is true with its behavior management efforts. As uncomfortable as it may be, if you truly want to dramatically improve the learning environment at your school, you must start by taking a good, hard look at exactly where you are as you begin the process.

The Data You Need

You will need solid data on areas such as the following:

- The behavior management issues that concern the staff
- Student referrals to the office
- Areas of the school where problem behaviors occur

The Benefits of Data-Driven Behavior Management Efforts

Why are good data so important? Good data do the following:

- Support the ability to quickly respond to chronic and severe behavior problems
- Enable you to identify staff members who need additional training
- Help you determine when modification of the schoolwide efforts is needed

Through data you will be able to determine, in general, what is working with the schoolwide plan and what needs to be changed. There is no way a schoolwide plan should be cast in stone.

All Staff Are Accountable to Implement the Schoolwide Behavior Management Plan

The staff of effective schools recognizes the old adage, "A chain is only as strong as its weakest link." In other words, all staff members are expected to buy in to the schoolwide management efforts and present a united front to the students (Taylor-Greene et al., 1997).

No schoolwide plan will ever work if staff are allowed to choose whether or not they feel like supporting it. Through the efforts of the behavior management committee and the administration, all members of the staff need to be motivated to actively support the schoolwide plan.

Steps to Ensure Staff Accountability

How can you get all the staff at a school on the same page when it comes to implementing the schoolwide behavior efforts? In reality, it is very similar to the steps it takes to motivate students to choose to follow the schoolwide behavior plan.

Clearly Communicate Expectations. First, the behavior management committee must clearly state their expectations for how they believe the staff has to deal with the students' behavior and support the school's behavior management plan. Through both words and actions they will establish clear guidelines for how each and every staff person, no matter what his or her position, will respond to student behavior (Colvin, 2007). These may be similar to those listed in the section on skills staff members need to deal with student behavior in chapter 9, "Effectively Communicate Explicit Directions," on page 57.

Provide Positive Support. Second, the committee members and the administrators will provide consistent, positive feedback to any and all staff that support the school's behavior management plan. This may take the form of verbal recognition of the staff member, public recognition at staff meetings or in the bulletin, or special incentives such as taking over a classroom and giving the teacher an extra prep period.

Provide Assistance and Corrective Feedback. Finally, there is no way a committee member or administrator will sit back if they see or hear of staff letting the little things slide. Quick action will be the name of the game. In addition, any staff member who is underperforming will be offered additional training and assistance to increase their professional competence.

If the additional assistance is not effective, the administration will step in and, clearly and firmly, let the staff member know they have a choice: improve how they support the school's plan and how they deal with students or they will have to consider working at another school.

There are no words that can express how critical it is that the school has an administrator who will hold staff accountable to perform. Without such accountability, schoolwide efforts will soon wane and fail.

> ## ▶ Key Points to Remember ◀
>
> Schoolwide implementation of the concepts and strategies found in the Assertive Discipline program can support a staff member's efforts to turn around the learning environment at their school. Effective implementation includes the following:
>
> - Staff members who raise their expectations for student behavior
> - Administrators who walk the walk
> - A behavior management committee that guides all efforts
> - A comprehensive, research-based schoolwide behavior management plan
> - Staff trained to utilize Assertive Discipline strategies
> - Data-driven effort
> - Staff members who are fully accountable and fully support the schoolwide behavior management plan

References and Resources

Algozzine, B., & Ysseldyke, J. (2006). *Effective instruction for students with special needs: A practical guide for every teacher.* Thousand Oaks, CA: Corwin Press.

Arlin, M. (1979). Teacher transitions can disrupt time flow in classroom. *American Educational Research Journal, 16*(1), 42–56.

Brophy, J. (1996). *Teaching problem students.* New York: Guilford Press.

Brophy, J., & Evertson, C. M. (1976). *Learning from teaching: A developmental perspective.* Boston: Allyn & Bacon.

Burden, P. R. (2000). *Powerful classroom management strategies: Motivating students to learn.* Thousand Oaks, CA: Corwin Press.

Canter, L. (2006). *Classroom management for academic success.* Bloomington, IN: Solution Tree Press.

Canter, L., & Canter, M. (1976). *Assertive discipline: A take charge approach for today's educator* (1st ed.). Santa Monica, CA: Canter and Associates.

Canter, L., & Canter, M. (1992). *Assertive discipline: Positive behavior management for today's classroom* (2nd ed.). Santa Monica, CA: Canter and Associates.

Canter, L., & Canter, M. (1993). *Succeeding with difficult students: New strategies for reaching your most challenging students.* Santa Monica, CA: Canter and Associates.

Canter, L., & Canter, M. (2001a). *Assertive discipline: Positive behavior management for today's classroom* (3rd ed.). Santa Monica, CA: Canter and Associates.

Canter, L., & Canter, M. (2001b). *Parents on your side: A teacher's guide to creating positive relationships with parents* (2nd ed.). Los Angeles: Canter and Associates.

Canter, L., & Peterson, K. (1996). *Teaching students to get along.* Santa Monica, CA: Canter and Associates.

Charles, C. M. (1999). *Building classroom discipline* (6th ed.). New York: Longman.

Charles, C. M. (2000). *The synergetic classroom: Joyful teaching and gentle discipline.* New York: Longman.

Chui, L., & Tulley, M. (1997). Student preferences of teacher discipline styles. *Journal of Instructional Psychology, 24*(3), 169–175.

Cipriano Pepperl, J., & Lezotte, L. (2001). *High expectations.* Okemos, MI: Effective Schools Products.

Colvin, G. (2007). *7 steps for developing a proactive schoolwide discipline plan.* Thousand Oaks, CA: Corwin Press.

Colvin, G., & Lazar, M. (1997). *The effective elementary classroom: Managing for success.* Longmont, CO: Sopris West.

Cotton, K. (1990). *School improvement series. Close-up #9: Schoolwide and classroom discipline.* Portland, OR: Northwest Regional Educational Laboratory.

Curwin, R., & Mendler, A. (1998). *Discipline with dignity.* Alexandria, VA: Association for Supervision and Curriculum Development.

Di Giulio, R. (2004). *Great teaching.* Thousand Oaks, CA: Corwin Press.

Dweck, C. (2007). *Mind set: The new psychology of success.* New York: Ballantine Books.

Education Trust. (2006). *Yes we can: Telling truths and dispelling myths about race and education in America.* Washington, DC: Author.

Emmer, E. T., & Hickman, J. (1991). Teacher efficacy in classroom management and discipline. *Educational and Psychological Measurement, 51*(3), 755–765.

Emmer, E. T., Sanford, J. P., Clements, B. S., & Martin, J. (1982). *Improving classroom management and organization in junior high schools: An experimental investigation.* Austin, TX: Research and Development Center for Teacher Education, University of Texas (R & D Report No. 6153). (ERIC Document Reproduction Service No. ED261053)

Emmer, E. T., Sanford, J. P., Evertson, C. M., Clements, B. S., & Martin, J. (1981). *The classroom management improvement study: An experiment in elementary school classrooms.* Austin, TX: Research and Development Center for Teacher Education, University of Texas (R & D Report No. 6050). (ERIC Document Reproduction Service No. ED226452)

Epstein, J. L., Clark, L., Salinas, K. C., & Sanders, M. G. (1997). *Scaling up school-family-community connections in Baltimore: Effects on student achievement and attendance.* Paper presented at the annual meeting of the American Educational Research Association, Chicago, IL.

Evertson, C., & Harris, A. (1997). *COMP classroom organization and management program.* Nashville, TN: Vanderbilt University.

Gibbs, N. (2005). Parents behaving badly. *Time, 165*(8), 40–49.

Gladwell, M. (2002). *The tipping point: How little things can make a big difference.* New York: Back Bay Books.

Good, T., & Brophy, J. (2003). *Looking in classrooms* (9th ed.). Boston: Allyn & Bacon.

Gordon, D. T. (1999, September/October). Rising to the discipline challenge. *Harvard Education Letter,* 1–4.

Harmin, M., & Toth., M. (2006). *Inspiring active learning: A complete handbook for today's teachers.* Alexandria, VA: Association for Supervision and Curriculum Development.

Heim, P. (2001). Video program five: Engage all learners' presentation skills. In *Motivating today's learner* (pp. 41–47). Santa Monica, CA: Canter and Associates.

Henderson, A., & Mapp, K. (2002). *A new wave of evidence: The impact of school, family, and community connections on student achievement.* Austin, TX: Southwest Educational Development Laboratory.

Horner, R., Sugai, G., Eber, L., & Lewandowski, H. (2004). *Illinois positive behavior interventions and support project: 2003-2004 progress report.* University of Oregon: Center on Positive Behavioral Interventions and Supports Illinois State Board of Education.

Horner, R. H., Sugai, G., Todd, A. W., & Lewis-Palmer, T. (2005). School-wide positive behavior support: An alternative approach to discipline in schools. In L. M. Bambara & L. Lern (Eds.), *Individualized supports for students with problem behaviors* (pp. 359–390). New York: Guilford Press.

James, A. (2007). *Teaching the male brain: How boys think, feel, and learn in school.* Thousand Oaks, CA: Corwin Press.

Jenson, W., Rhode, G., Evans, C., & Morgan, D. (2006). *The tough kid principal's briefcase.* Boston: Sopris West.

Jiménez, T. C., & Graf, V. L. (2008). *Education for all: Critical issues in the education of children and youth with disabilities.* San Francisco: Jossey-Bass.

Johnson, D., Maruyama, G., Johnson, R., Nelson, D., & Skon, L. (1981). Effects of cooperative, competitive, and individualistic goal structures on achievement: A meta-analysis. *Psychological Bulletin, 89*(1), 47–62.

Johnson, J. (2004, June 23). Why is school discipline considered a trivial issue? *Education Week, 23*(41), 48.

Jones, F. (2000). *Tools for teaching.* Santa Cruz, CA: Fred H. Jones & Associates.

Jones, L., & Jones, V. (2004). *Comprehensive classroom management: Creating communities of support and solving problems* (7th ed.). Boston: Allyn & Bacon.

Kam, C. M., Greenberg, M. T., & Walls, C. T. (2003). Examining the role of implementation quality in school-based prevention using the PATHS curriculum. *Prevention Science, 4*(1), 55–63.

Kerman, S., Kimball, T., & Martin, M. (1980). Teacher expectations and student achievement. *Phi Delta Kappan, 61*(9), 119–128.

Kohn, A. (1993). *Punished by rewards.* Boston: Houghton Mifflin.

Kounin, J. (1970). *Discipline and group management in classrooms.* New York: Holt, Rinehart and Winston.

LaFleur, L. H., Witt, J. C., Naquin, G., Harwell, V., & Gilbertson, D. (1998). Use of coaching to enhance proactive classroom management by improvement of student transitioning between classroom activities. *Effective School Practices, 17*(2), 70–82.

Lane, K. L., Givner, C. C., & Pierson, M. R. (2004, July). Teacher expectations of student behavior: Social skills necessary for success in elementary school classrooms. *Journal of Special Education, 38*(2), 104–110.

Langdon, C. (1996). The third Gallup/Phi Delta Kappa poll of teachers' attitudes toward the public schools. *Phi Delta Kappan, 78*(3), 244–250.

Levin, J., & Shaken-Kaye, J. (2001). *The self-control classroom: Understanding and managing the disruptive behavior of all students.* Dubuque, IA: Kendall Hunt.

Lewis, T., & Sugai, G. (1999, February). Effective behavior support: A systems approach to proactive schoolwide management. *Focus on Exceptional Children, 31*, 1–24.

Luiselli, J. K., Putnam, R. F., Handler, M. W., & Feinberg, A. B. (2005). Whole-school positive behavior support: Effects on student discipline problems and academic performance. *Educational Psychology, 25*(2/3), 183–198.

MacKenzie, R. (1996). *Setting limits in the classroom: How to move beyond the classroom dance of discipline.* Roseville, CA: Prima.

Marzano, R., Marzano J., & Pickering, D. (2003).*Classroom management that works: Research-based strategies for every teacher.* Alexandria, VA: Association for Supervision and Curriculum Development.

Mendler, A. (2001). *Connecting with students.* Alexandria, VA: Association for Supervision and Curriculum Development.

Mendler, A., & Curwin, R. (1999). *Discipline with dignity for challenging youth.* Bloomington, IN: Solution Tree Press (formerly National Educational Service).

Metropolitan Life Insurance Co. (2005). *The MetLife survey of the American teacher 2004–2005.* New York: Author.

Muller, C. (2001). The role of caring in the teacher-student relationship for at-risk students. *Sociological Inquiry, 71*(2), 241–255.

Public Agenda. (2004). *Teaching interrupted: Do discipline policies in today's public schools foster the common good?* Accessed at www.publicagenda.org/reports/teaching-interrupted on September 24, 2009.

Quaglia, R. (2008). *My aspiration survey.* Portland, ME: Quaglia Institute for Student Aspirations.

Reid, J. B., Patterson, G. R., & Snyder, J. J. (Eds.). (2002). *Antisocial behavior in children and adolescents: A developmental analysis and the Oregon model for intervention.* Washington, DC: American Psychological Association.

Riegler, H., & Baer, D. (1989). A developmental analysis of rule-following. *Advances in Child Development and Behavior, 21,* 191–219.

Rogers, S. (2001). *Teaching tips.* Evergreen, CO: Peak Learning Systems.

Rosenthal, R. (1974). *On the social psychology of the self-fulfilling prophecy: Further evidence for Pygmalion effects and their mediating mechanisms.* New York: MSS Modular Publications.

Rowe, M. (1986). Wait time: Slowing down may be a way of speeding up! *Journal of Teacher Education, 37*(1), 43–50.

Sadker, M., & Sadker, D. (1994). *Failing at fairness: How America's schools cheat girls.* New York: Scribner's.

Savage, T. V., & Savage, M. K. (2008). *Successful classroom management and discipline: Teaching self-control and responsibility.* Thousand Oaks, CA: Sage.

Scheeler, M. (2004). Providing performance feedback to teachers: A review. *Teacher Education and Special Education, 27*(4), 396–407.

Scheeler, M. (2006). Effects of corrective feedback delivered via wireless technology on preservice teacher performance and student behavior. *Teacher Education and Special Education, 29*(1), 12–25.

Scott, T. M., & Barrett, S. B. (2004). Using staff and student time engaged in disciplinary procedures to evaluate the impact of school-wide PBS. *Journal of Positive Behavior Interventions, 6*(1), 21–27.

Smith, R. (2004). *Conscious classroom management: Unlocking the secrets of great teaching.* San Rafael, CA: Conscious Teaching Publications.

Sprague, J., & Golly, A. (2005). *Best behavior: Building positive behavior support in schools.* Longmont, CO: Sopris West.

Sprague, J. R., Sugai, G., & Walker, H. (1998). Antisocial behavior in schools. In T. S. Watson & F. M. Gresham (Eds.), *Handbook of child behavior therapy* (pp. 451–474). New York: Plenum.

Sprague, J., & Walker, H. (2005). *Safe and healthy schools: Practical prevention strategies.* New York: Guilford Press.

Sprick, R., Garrison, M., & Howard, L. (1998). *CHAMPs: A proactive approach to classroom management.* Longmont, CO: Sopris West.

Sprick, R., Knight, J., Reinke, W., & McKale, T. (2006). *Coaching classroom management: Strategies and tools for administrators and coaches.* Eugene, OR: Pacific Northwest Publishing.

Stage, S. A., & Quiroz, D. R. (1997). A meta-analysis of interventions to decrease disruptive classroom behavior in public education settings. *School Psychology Review, 26*(3), 333–368.

Strayhorn, T. L. (2008, May). Teacher expectations and urban black males' success in school: Implications for academic leaders. *Academic Leadership, 6*(2). Accessed at www.academicleadership.org/emprical_research on July 19, 2009.

Sugai, G., Horner, R., & Gresham, F. (2002). Behaviorally effective school environments. In M. Shinn, H. Walker, & G. Stoner (Eds.), *Interventions for academic and behavior problems II: Preventive and remedial approaches* (pp. 315–350). Bethesda, MD: National Association of School Psychologists.

Tauber, R. (1999). *Classroom management: Sound theory and effective practice.* Westport, CT: Bergin & Garvey.

Tauber, R., & Mester, C. (2006). *Acting lessons for teachers: Using performance skills in the classroom* (2nd ed.). New York: Praeger.

Taylor-Greene, S., Brown, D., Nelson, L., Longton, J., Gassman, T., Cohen, J., Swartz, J., Horner, R. H., Sugai, G., & Hall, S. (1997). School-wide behavioral support: Starting the year off right. *Journal of Behavioral Education, 7*(1), 99–112.

Van Houten, R. (1980). *Learning through feedback.* New York: Human Sciences Press.

Walker, H., Colvin, G., & Ramsey, E. (1995). *Antisocial behavior in school: Strategies and best practices.* Pacific Grove, CA: Brooks/Cole.

Walker, H., Ramsey, E., & Gresham, F. (2004). *Antisocial behavior in school: Evidence-based practices* (2nd ed.). Belmont, CA: Wadsworth/Thomson.

Walker, H., & Walker, J. (1991). *Coping with noncompliance in the classroom: A positive approach for teachers.* Austin, TX: Pro-Ed.

Walker, H. M., & Eaton-Walker, J. (2000, March). Key questions about school safety: Critical issues and recommended solutions. *NASSP Bulletin,* 46–55.

Wang, M. C., Haertel, G. D., & Walberg, H. J. (1993). Toward a knowledge base for school learning. *Review of Educational Research, 63*(3), 249–294.

Watson, M. (2003). *Learning to trust.* San Francisco: Jossey-Bass.

Weinstein, R. S., & McKown, C. (1998). Expectancy effects in "context": Listening to the voices of students and teachers. In J. Brophy (Ed.), *Advances in research on teaching: Expectations in the classroom* (vol. 7, pp. 215–242). Greenwich, CT: JAI Press.

Whitaker, T. (2004). *What great teachers do differently.* Poughkeepsie, NY: Eye on Education.

Witt, J., LaFleur, L., Naquin, G., & Gilbertson, D. (1999). *Teaching effective classroom routines.* Longmont, CO: Sopris West.

Wong, K., & Wong, R. (1998). *First days of school: How to be an effective teacher.* Mountain View, CA: Harry K. Wong Publications.

Wright, S. P., Horn, S. P., & Sanders, W. L. (1997). Teacher and classroom context effects on student achievement: Implications for teacher evaluation. *Journal of Personnel Evaluation in Education, 11*(1), 57–67.

Index

A

administrator(s)
    classroom management plan, giving to, 38, 120
    sending student to, 76
    support from, 6, 25, 120, 127–129
anger
    handling student, 76–79
    showing your, 12
arguing with students, 12–13, 75–77
assertive tone, 10
attention-getting signals, 60
authority, lack of respect for, 3–4

B

backup plans, need for, 77–78
behavioral narration, 27, 63
    benefits of, 64–67
    classwide reward system and, 68–69
    how to use, 64
    motivating students to get on task with, 67–70
    one-minute rule, 69–70, 101
    points to remember, 70
    teacher voice, use of, 5, 9–13, 67
    two-second rule, 67
behavior awards, 28
behavior curriculum
    determine order for teaching content, 47
    points to remember, 55
    teacher responsible behavior lesson list, 54–55
behavior curriculum, elementary-level
    beginning-of-the-day procedures, 49, 50
    classroom management plan, 48
    classroom space, use of, 49
    cooperative group work, 50–51
    ending the day and leaving the classroom, 49, 50
    independent work, 49, 51
    learning centers, work at, 51
    outdoor management, 49
    partner work, 50
    student comfort and safety issues, 48
    teaching students to pay attention, 48
behavior curriculum, secondary-level
    beginning-of-the-day procedures, 52, 53
    classroom management plan, 51
    classroom space, use of, 52
    cooperative group work, 53–54
    ending the period and leaving the classroom, 52
    independent work, 52
    lab work, 54
    partner work, 53
    student comfort and safety issues, 52
    teaching students to pay attention, 51
Behavior Management Cycle, 57
    behavioral narration, 63–70

behavior plans, individualized, 115–118
classroom management structure, 81–87
corrective actions, taking, 71–79
directions, giving explicit, 58–61
engagement strategies, 89–102
behavior plans, individualized, 115–118
bird walking, 100
broken-window theory, 143–144

C

choral responses, 93–94
classroom management
    demographics, impact of changing, 4
    importance of, 3
    lack of training in, 4–5
classroom management structure
    highly structured (level one), 82–83
    levels of, 81–82
    points to remember, 87
    recalibrating, 86
    self-management, moving toward (level two), 84–85
    self-management, reaching (level three), 85–86
    sharing with parents and administrators, 120, 121
classroom managers, attributes of effective
    discipline plan in place, 6
    high expectations for student behavior, 6
    motivation strategies, 6
    positive relationships with students, 6
    strong teacher voice, 5
    student behavior policies and procedures, 6
    support from parents and administrators, 6
coercive, difference between corrective and, 33
compliance, defined, 4–5
cornerstone behavior, 73
corrective actions
    anger and defiance, handling student, 76–79
    back-up plans, need for, 77–78
    difference between coercive and, 33
    examples of, 34–35
    how to plan and use, 34–35, 37–38
    keeping track of, 36–37
    organized in a hierarchy, 35–36, 72, 83, 84, 85, 86
    points to remember, 38, 79
    reasons for using, 33
    severe clause, 36
    students' testing of teachers, 74–79
    student who refuses to leave the classroom, 77–78
    taking, 71–79
    talking, handling inappropriate, 73–74

D

defiant students
    handling, 76–79
    never back down, 18

demographics, impact of changing, 4
detentions, use of, 35
directions, explicit
    attention-getting signals, 60
    checking for understanding, 60
    cuing students, 61
    difference between vague directions and, 58
    how to communicate, 60–61
    how to determine, for an activity, 59–60
    participation in activities, 59–60
    physical movement, 59
    points to remember, 61
    restating, 72
    verbal behavior, 59
discipline plan, 6
    See also corrective actions
    advantages of, 24–25, 143–154
    attributes of effective, 146–154
    components of, 23
    development of, 25–26
    difference between observable and unclear rules, 26
    goal of, 23
    implementing a, 146
    importance of following through with, 15
    ineffective, reasons for, 143–145
    points to remember, 26, 154
    rules need to be applicable all day/period, 26
    sample of, for elementary students, 23–24
    sample of, for secondary students, 24
    student input, 26
disruptive behavior
    documenting, 120, 121
    ineffective responses to, 11–12
    motivation and, 27
    never back down, 18
    no excuses for, 16–17
    small stuff, dealing with the, 17–18
    students with ADHD or autism, 17
    teacher voice to correct, 12
documenting disruptive behavior, 120, 121

E

elementary students
    behavior curriculum for, 48–51
    corrective actions for, 35–36
    discipline plan for, 23–24
    special privileges for, 28
engagement strategies
    choral responses, 93–94
    enthusiasm, use of, 96–99
    lesson pacing, 99–100
    momentum, maintaining, 100–101
    opportunities to respond, providing, 89–90
    pair share, 95–96
    points to remember, 102
    questioning, 90–93
    quick write, 95
    voting, 94–95
enthusiasm, use of, 96–99
    eye contact, 98
    gestures, 98
    movement, 98
    teaching with, 96–99
    vocal volume and pace, 97–100
explicit directions. *See* directions, explicit

F

feedback
    See also behavioral narration
    bug in the ear, 136–137
    real-time, 137–139
    verbal, 116

H

high expectations
    as an attribute, 6
    high-stakes testing days and, 20–21
    never back down, 18
    no excuses for disruptive behavior, 16–18
    100 percent compliance with directions
        100 percent of the time, 15–16
    points to remember, 21
    praise, avoiding excessive, 19–20
    small stuff, dealing with the, 17–18
home-school behavior contract, 126–127
home visits, 123
hostile tone, 10

I

incentives, timed, 83
individualized behavior plans, 115–118
Individuals with Disabilities Education Act (IDEA), 4

L

lesson pacing, 99–100

M

motivation, 6
    behavior awards, 28
    classwide, 29–30
    impact on disruptive behavior, 27
    for individual students, 27–28
    parents, involving, 27–28
    peer pressure and, 29
    points-on-the-board reward system, 29–31
    points to remember, 31
    special privileges, 28
    verbal recognition, 27
myth of the good teacher, 119–120

N

nagging, 11–12
No Child Left Behind Act, 4
nonassertive voice, 9
noncompliance, defined, 5
nonverbal communication, 72

O

observable rules, difference between unclear rules and, 26
one-minute rule, 69–70
opportunities to respond, providing, 89–90

P

pace busters, 100
pair share, 95–96
parents
    calls to, 35
    classroom management plan letter to, 120, 121
    conferences with, 124–126

home visits, 123
  sending positive notes/phone calls to, 27–28, 123
  support from, 6, 25, 120–127
peer pressure, motivation and, 29
physical movement, 59
points-on-the-board reward system, 29–31, 83
policies and procedures
  determining, 39–41
  responsible behavior, planning a lesson on, 41–44
  responsible behavior lesson format, 44–46
positive support. *See* motivation
praise
  avoiding excessive, 19–20
  problem with using, 65–66
privileges, special, 28

Q

questions
  common mistakes teachers make when asking, 90–91
  techniques to use when asking, 91–93
  quick write, 95

R

Real Time Classroom Coaching Model, 13
  advantages of, 139–141
  description of, 131, 133–139
  points to remember, 142
recalibrating, 86
recognition, 19
Rehabilitation Act (1973), 4
responsible behavior
  examples of, 42–44
  have students practice, 46
  lesson format, 44–46
  modeling, 45
  planning a lesson on, 41–44
  points to remember, 46
rules
  See also discipline plan
  difference between observable and unclear, 26

S

secondary students
  behavior curriculum for, 51–54
  corrective actions for, 36
  discipline plan for, 24
  special privileges for, 28
self-management, moving toward (level two), 84–85
self-management, reaching (level three), 85–86
severe clause, 36
small stuff, dealing with the, 17–18, 73–74
student behavior
  anger and defiance, handling, 76–79
  correcting disruptive behavior with teacher voice, 11–12
  discipline plan's benefits on, 24–25
  high expectations for, 6, 15–21
  policies and procedures on, 6
  refuses to leave the classroom, 77–78
  talking, handling inappropriate, 73–74
  teacher voice to recognize appropriate, 11
students
  anger, showing your, 12

arguing with, 12–13, 75–76
how they test teachers, 74–79
rule development and input from, 26
talking during lesson, how to handle, 11
trusting relationships with, 6, 103–105
student-teacher relationships
  authenticity, 108
  importance of learning about the students, 106–107
  letting students get to know you, 108
  listening to students, 107
  mistakes, admitting, 108
  points to remember, 113
  reaching out/contacting students, methods for, 108–113
  respect, 106
  trust, 6, 103–105
support
  See also motivation
  administrator, 6, 25, 120, 127–129
  parental, 6, 25, 120–127
  points to remember, 129
  struggling teachers, 142

T

talking, handling inappropriate, 73–74
teachers' authority, lack of respect for, 3–4
teacher voice
  arguing with students, 12–13
  attributes of, 5, 10–13
  behavioral narration and use of, 67
  correcting disruptive behavior with, 11–12
  defined, 9
  difference between a nonassertive voice and, 9
  fills the room, 10
  how to develop a, 13
  importance of, 9
  never speak over students, 11
  points to remember, 13
  recognizing appropriate student behavior with, 11
  tone, assertive versus hostile, 10
teaching style, assessing your, 98–99
ten-to-twenty-second rule, 71–72
Think Sheet, 34–35
threatening, 12
time outs, 34
trusting relationships, creating, 6, 103–105
two-second rule, 67

U

unclear rules, difference between observable rules and, 26

V

verbal behavior, 59
verbal feedback, 116
verbal recognition, 27
  See also behavioral narration
verbal reinforcement, 19
visual aids, use of, 41
voting, 94–95

W

withitness, 150

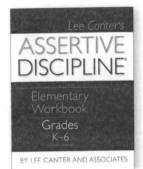

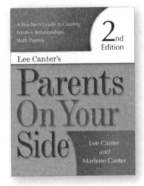